Date Due			
Morse			
Staff			
Hutch			

780.9   Marquis, G. Welton
M

         Yes Sir, That's My
     Wolfgang

YES SIR, THAT'S MY WOLFGANG

An

Irreverent History

of

Music

By

G. Welton Marquis

PRENTICE-HALL, Inc.

Englewood Cliffs, New Jersey

Decorative chapter opening initials from
Decorative Initials and Alphabets
by Alexander Nesbitt.
Dover Publications, Inc., New York, 1959.
Reprinted through permission of the publisher.

Yes Sir, That's My Wolfgang: An Irreverent History of Music, by
G. Welton Marquis

Library of Congress Catalog Card Number: 67-18922

Printed in the United States of America

T 97220

Prentice-Hall International, Inc., *London*
Prentice-Hall of Australia, Pty. Ltd., *Sydney*
Prentice-Hall of Canada, Ltd., *Toronto*
Prentice-Hall of India Private Ltd., *New Delhi*
Prentice-Hall of Japan, Inc., *Tokyo*

To
GRETA
for her
drawings
and
understanding

PREFACE

For many years, colleges and universities in North America and Europe have offered music history and so-called "music appreciation" courses in the hope of introducing young men and women to the many cultural aspects of music. In addition, publishers have bombarded citizens of all countries with innumerable books related to music: the stories of operas; how to distinguish symphonies from symphonic poems; boys' lives of Mozart and Schubert; historical novels concerning composers with romantic proclivities, and hundreds of other books dealing with romanticized facets of music history. Much good has resulted from this.

Nevertheless, this writer has felt that something was lacking; profundity, perhaps. It is barely possible that facts concerning the history of music have been coated with the gloss of superficiality; that is, writers and publishers—and even some teachers —have underestimated the ability of the world-wide reading public to absorb musical truths, even though these truths be cold and startling in their impact upon one's stream of consciousness.

After teaching beginning and graduate courses in music appreciation over a period of fifty-seven years, this writer has arrived at the conclusion that the average person still does not know the difference between a symphony and a symphonic poem. And in fact, even those students who study music for professional purposes do not realize that Chopin actually did do some composing on the island of Majorca during his sojourn there with George Sand.

Needless to say, this present book is written as a remedy. It is written for the sole purpose of bridging hiatuses. It is written in the spirit of that great Greek historian, Thucydides, who wrote as follows:

> The lack of the fabulous may make my work dull. But I shall be satisfied if it be thought useful by those who wish to know the exact character of events now past which, human nature being what it is, will recur in a similar or analogous form. It has not been composed to court temporary applause but as a lasting possession.

Like Thucydides, this writer realizes that the very profundity of his thinking may make his work "dull" to superficial minds, but he maintains that any citizen of the United States of America has the right (if not a duty) to know that a sackbut does not resemble a krummhorn, and that Richard the Lion-Hearted performed on neither instrument well, chiefly because neither instrument had been invented at the time of his life. The youth of North America—and indeed, of all continents—will be able to adjust better in a democratic society if they realize that Johann Sebastian Bach fathered twenty children and still had time to compose a prodigious amount of music for people owning high fidelity phonographs. The readers of this book will discover that their forefathers were never too busy to be fathers.

During his fifty-seven years of teaching, this writer has also discovered that the average college or university student is less interested in hearing Franz Liszt's *Sonata in B Minor* than about the composer's relationships with the opposite sex. This book does not intend to destroy that scholarly enthusiasm.

And lastly, too little attention has been paid to music written before Bach, that is, before 1700. Certainly this is most serious.

True, some books on music appreciation and history "suggest" that music did exist prior to this date, and a few even devote a page or two to Greek and Roman music. However, this is far from being enough. No young man or woman should be allowed to graduate from any accredited university without a detailed knowledge of music in the Pleistocene era, and yet this information is frequently omitted from music texts.

It is, for example, ridiculous for educators to state that we are training young men and women to assume roles in society, and yet neglect to train these identical young men and women to differentiate between Pleistocene and Pliocene music. Educators must stop to ponder their responsibilities in this age of quiz programs. Needless to say, a participant unable to state succinctly and without hesitation that the first bone·flute was manufactured in 998,764 B.C. by a twenty-four-year-old member of the *Homo modjokertensis* clan in Java (and that this flute overblew at an interval of the seventeenth), will find it almost impossible to adjust to our modern society. Such men and women will exist in a void of ignorance that will be demonstrated most vividly at the breakfast table. Such conversational impotence will, of course, wreak havoc on their children.

This writer knows, therefore, that this book will fill a real need, and if it has inadequacies, these may be remedied in turn by candidates for the Ph.D. degree in Music who will find innumerable dissertation topics in the following pages. Such candidates are cautioned, however, to remember that most doctoral dissertations result from a careful perusal of footnotes, many of which are included in this edition. A great number of diagrams, musical examples and pictures are also included for those readers who own pump organs or five-string banjos, and who like to look at diagrams and pictures.

All readers must realize that a book such as this must, of necessity, be scholarly and serious, for as Mark Twain said, humor is out of place in a dictionary. This book then will treat *Pithecanthropus erectus*, Richard the Lion-Hearted, and the sackbut with understandable dignity; it will also discuss the mistresses of composers with a combination of dignity and envy. It is to be hoped that readers will read about these grave matters in the same way.

This writer, above all, wishes to acknowledge his immense debt of gratitude to his doctoral professor, Dr. Hugo Steinglissinger, who was the original source of stimulation and wellspring for all that this writer knows about musical matters. Indeed, Dr. Steinglissinger's gargantuan output of monographs, editions, and articles provides much of the scholarly confirmation for facts found in this present book.

This writer would also like to thank the various libraries, museums, and department stores that allowed him to quote without charge from their copyright holdings. And lastly, due acknowledgement must be made to those loyal students in this writer's many seminars on music history and appreciation for their excellence in writing chapters one through twenty. If they receive no money for this they will, at least, realize that this writer will cherish their loyalties forever.

George Welton Marquis
Vancouver, Canada

CONTENTS

1

EOCENE
MUSIC

he music of the Eocene period is customarily divided into early (Paleocene), middle (Eocene), and later (Oligocene).[1] Since the Paleocene period began 60,000,001 years ago,[2] very little of its music has survived the ravages of time, and the few folk tunes that have come down to us through word of mouth are unharmonized and thus throw little light on the matter.[3]

The few extant musical fragments, however, enable us to say with scholarly determination that the music of the Paleocene period was not notable for its high development of counterpoint and harmony regardless of Edelweiss-Schlimmerpumpf's insinuations. Furthermore, the string quartet of Bridgette Hissen-

[1] Hugo Steinglissinger, *Die älteste eocaenische Musik*, vol. 251, p. 7,354. Even Dr. Steinglissinger did not know why the middle part of the Eocene period was also the Eocene, but as he said, "It's no use crying over spilt milk: it only makes it salty for the cat."

[2] *Ibid.*, p. 9,431. But see Schmidtfuss's treatise on this matter. He maintains that the Paleocene period began 60,000,002 years ago. Needless to say, Schmidtfuss cannot be trusted.

[3] But see Edelweiss-Schlimmerpumpf who bristles at such a suggestion. As he wrote in his well-known preface, "Be thou as chaste as ice, as pure as snow, thou shalt not escape calumny."

baum is nowhere to be seen and thus lies far in the future. Or as Dr. Steinglissinger pointed out, *"Es ist nicht da!"* [4] As a matter of fact, recent research indicates that man did not exist either during this period, or as Dr. Steinglissinger stated with such profundity, *"Er ist nicht da!"* [5]

This suggests that it may be some time before the football band and symphony will be invented, and that we should move on to the Eocene period when things will improve. Although the Eocene lasted from 49,999,999 B.C. to 30,000,004 B.C., it proves to be somewhat disappointing also due to the complete lack of musical examples—and man. However, we do know that the bassoon was invented in the year 43,000,008 B.C., since a fossilized bed post (the ancestor of the bassoon) was found in the famous Reading Beds of England during Heinrich Puffendorf's extensive excavations in the winter of 1836. [6]

After careful examination, it was found that this bed post had a range of one note if the performer pursed his lips hard. However, Dr. Puffendorf discovered over a period of twenty-seven years that this range could be extended by inserting the thumb of the left hand in the bottom opening of the bed post. Thus, the instrument's complete range is as follows:

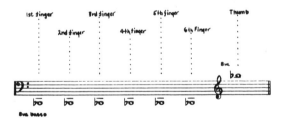

[4] Hugo Steinglissinger, *Studien über die älteste eocaenische Musik und Studien zur Tonartenlehre des frühen Altertumes*, vol. 746, p. 2,347. In the English translation of this vital edition, the above conclusion is rendered rather clumsily as, "It is not there!"

[5] *Ibid.*, p. 10,398. Doctoral candidates should note that Baumschmidt disagrees, but he is not highly regarded in academic circles.

[6] The year of the dense fog which prompted Dr. Puffendorf to compose the following immortal lines: "I wandered lonely as a cloud that floats on high o'er vales and hills."

Leonardo da Vinci's famous drawing of this fossilized bed post is as follows, complete with the original double reed.

Although it has been indicated above that the Oligocene period is frequently considered to be the late stage of the Eocene, music historians (with a few notorious exceptions) [7] prefer to treat it as a separate period. This is due chiefly to the appearance of the little four-toed horse, or Eohippus, which served as a modest inspiration to various composers of the Oligocene.

Unfortunately, no Oligocene compositions have come down to us, but miraculously enough a pen and ink portrait of the pe-

[7] Schnorkel, Braundesserdorf, Kempelssohn, Fliegerregenschmidt, Bach (*not* Johann Sebastian), and Hesselwurst. It should be noted, however, that young music scholars must approach these men with caution, as they are not reliable. Hesselwurst, in particular, has the reputation as an unbelievably stubborn person and his book is still used (lamentably) as a basic music appreciation text in certain unnamed institutions.

riod's principal composer, Groat van Lymph, has been pre-served. The instrument that he holds is, of course, a bone flute made from his uncle's left tibia.

The left hind foot of an Eohippus may be illustrated as follows.[8]

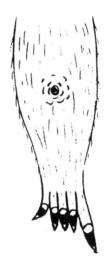

Omar Khayyam was the first scholar to bemoan the fact that football-band marches were not invented during the Eocene period, but there was, nevertheless, great hope in his heart when he wrote the immortal words: "Down my cheeks bitter tears incessant rain, and my heart struggles with convulsive sighs."

[8] From Dr. Steinglissinger's famous treatise, *Geschichte des Eohippuses,* Book One (*Füsse*), p. 750. See also Dr. Agnes Stoneslider's English translation of this book (*The History of Feet*). Unfortunately, one must admit that Dr. Stoneslider (Dr. Steinglissinger's youngest niece who emigrated to California in 1851) is not always reliable. Her illustration of the left hind foot of the Eohippus is marred by having the second toe from the left three centimeters too long, but as she said, "I am a lone lorn creetur, and everythink goes contrairy with me."

2

MIOCENE
MUSIC

he seas that had inundated the continents were beginning to recede during the Miocene period, and as one might surmise, composers tended to write for those instruments found in most abundance. It is therefore not surprising that the majority of compositions passed down to us from this period are scored for conch shells which must have been found on the beaches. This, of course, indicates that the old dissonances (unison and octave) had to be treated with exceptional care due to the tendency of conch shells to overblow at the interval of the minor second and, in fact, to play out of tune whether the performer purses his lips or not.[1]

---

[1] Otto Grossfuss, *Geschichte der oligocaenische Musik*, vol. 43, p. 798. Hermann Wagner (*not* Richard) disagrees, but his books do not sell well.

Extant paintings from this period indicate quite clearly that the conch shell was the preferred musical instrument.

In commenting on the development of Miocene music, the great American music historian, Oswald Twitch-feet, said: "Then gushed the tears from my eyes, through excess of regret, and flowed down my neck, till my sword-belt was drenched in the stream."

3

PLIOCENE
MUSIC

any reliable music historians omit the chapter on Pliocene music. The main reason is that man has not yet appeared.

Because of this, it seems doubtful if Pliocene composers contributed to the development of the basketball band or string quartet, so it may be best to move on to the next period when conditions are bound to improve.

Tannhauser Pflaumenguss summed up music developments in the Pliocene period stoutly and resolutely: "While old cats nibble cheese, the young ones learn."

4

PLEISTOCENE MUSIC

usic historians are still somewhat in doubt regarding the dating of the Pleistocene period, but it is expected that additional research will settle the issue. At the moment, we must be content with the very unscholarly guess that 1,000,001 B.C. is admissible as the starting point and that 8,002 B.C. may be acceptable as the end.[1] There are, however, a few music historians who maintain stoutly that the Pleistocene is merely one segment of the Quarternary, but such nonsense need not detain us in a scholarly book.[2]

There is, nevertheless, one thing of relative importance concerning this period, and that is the fact that we now encounter man. This is particularly cheering to the scholar who is interested in tracing the development of music for hockey bands and symphony orchestras, since despite the fact that music existed in the preceding eras, its development was hindered somewhat by two disturbing elements: (1) Dissonance (unison and octave) was treated in a stereotyped manner and was never resolved; and (2) Man did not exist.

[1] Kirchenpfeffer disagrees, but see Schmidt.
[2] Schmidt disagrees, but see Kirchenpfeffer.

In other words, pre-Pleistocene music was based for the most part on the reiteration of one note which may, or may not, have been doubled at the octave. This obviously did entail a certain amount of monotony, particularly in cadences.

However, with the appearance of man, that is, *Pithecanthropus erectus*, we find a new musical style being developed in Java. Here it is that we discover the true roots of that magnificent music composed later by Hermann von Süssenpfeiffer, Otto Nussbaum, and Bridgette Hissenbaum. This is, of course, heartening to the serious music historian.[3]

At one time (and some music history books continue the fiction),[4] it was believed that the primitive man, *Eoanthropus dawsoni*, was responsible for all this. A short composition, scored for two bone flutes (ulnas) and the jaw bone of a Baluchetherium, was found in a peat bog near the remains of a member of the *Eoanthropus dawsoni* tribe—known to us as the Piltdown Man. However, true musical scholars now know that *Eoanthropus dawsoni* never did exist and, in fact, is a fake—a fossilized forgery. Or as Kurt Schwindelsdorf said, "*Gut!*" [5]

We must not forget *Homo heidelbergensis*, however, since in the peat deposits near the present city of Heidelberg, a manuscript has been found scored for the femur of a saber-toothed tiger (which overblew at the augmented fourth), and the clavicle of an Etruscan rhinoceros.[6] The latter instrument is, of course, the ancestor of the clavichord.[7]

But most important is the fact that *Pithecanthropus erectus* invented the fugue and thus began that noble polyphonic form

---

[3] See Adolph Stumpf's magnificent collected works of *Pithecanthropus erectus* (*Pithecanthropus erectus: Sämtliche Werke*), vol. 367, p. 899, where he wrote, "You can fool some of the people all of the time, and all of the people some of the time, but you cannot fool all of the people all of the time."

[4] Pflaumenschmidt and Grossenbart, obviously.

[5] Kurt Schwindelsdorf, *Eine grosse Fake*, vol. 93, p. 7,629, fn. 78.

[6] Which possessed a hell of a range.

[7] The harpsichord derived its name from the Harpy, a Greek bird possessing dubious moral values.

that culminated with the compositions of Hermann von Süssenpfeiffer and his half-brother, Johann Sebastian Bach. In the following example, we see the beginning of one of these Pleistocene
fugues written for two index finger bones of an Asiatic lemur.[8]
It is, of course, astonishing to note the similarity between this
early work and Herman von Süssenpfeiffer's monumental fugue
for organ pedal. Both are even in the same key.

North American readers will note, of course, that their an-
cestors created no music during these early periods. Several reasons have been advanced for this, but at the moment it may be
only necessary to say that there were no men or women in
North America at that time.[9]

Thus, it appears that it may be some time before the lawn
bowling band or string sextet will be invented, so it seems best to
move on to the next period when things may improve.

> *Although the lawn bowling band did not appear during
> the Pleistocene era, Yancy Foss was not disheartened.
> An incurable optimist, he preferred to look ahead to
> future beauties: "Tear not from me then thy charms!
> Snatch, oh, snatch me to thine arms! With a life-in-
> spiring kiss, wake my sinking soul to bliss!"*

[8] Johannes Piffelschmidt, *Studien über die Finger*, vol. 97², p. 24,539.
In this work (*Studies about Fingers*) Dr. Piffelschmidt states further that
both of these index finger bones were on the lemur's left hand, although
he was prompt to say that most Pleistocene Asiatic lemurs had but one
index finger per hand. Grossenbauch insists that this fugue was written
for thumb bones, but his opinions are not held in high repute.

[9] Beissfluger, Braunschweiger, and Schmidt disagree, but their research
methods are suspect. However, as Beissfluger himself wrote, "A foolish
consistency is the hobgoblin of little minds."

5

POST-
PALAEOLITHIC
MUSIC

ith the disappearance of the great sheets of ice, we find ourselves in the Mesolithic period when tremendous musical developments will occur. Beginning on January 1, 8,000 B.C. all is changed. Gone are *Pithecanthropus erectus, Homo modjokertensis, Sinanthropus pekinensis, Eoanthropus dawsoni* (which never existed anyway, as we have seen), *Homo heidelbergensis, Homo neanderthalensis,* and the Cro-Magnons of France.

Gone too are the faithful seventy-five-foot animals these men kept as pets: the *Podokesaurus,* the *Struthiomimus,* the *Brontosaurus,* the *Diplodocus,* the *Brachiosaurus,* the *Stegosaurus,* the *Triceratops*—and even the *Protoceratops.* This is too bad, perhaps, but it was inevitable.[1]

Gone forever were these staunch friends of *Pithecanthropus erectus* and our only reminder of those glorious days are Dr. Grandtête's famous drawings. (Three are shown on the next page.)

---

[1] As Pierre Grandtête said, "The friendly cow all red and white, I love with all my heart. She gives me cream with all her might to eat with apple-tart."

The appearance of cats, dogs, chickens, horses and cows has left some scholars disconsolate, but we must remember what Hubert McGuire wrote in his History of Solace: "Into each life some rain must fall. Some days must be dark and dreary."

6

MUSIC
IN THE EARLY
EMPIRES

*abylonian Music.* In order to begin our slow but extremely scholarly journey toward future solace, we turn first to Babylonia where sometime between 1,146 and 1,123 B.C. Nebuchadnezzar I defeated the Elamites, but we hear nothing about military bands or string quartets. Another Nebuchadnezzar reigned from 605 to 561 B.C., but this simply illustrates the sordid fact that the Babylonians could not even think of new names for their children. They were exceedingly unimaginative, or as Horace Walpole wrote, " *Pfui!*" [1]

Assyrian Music

This nation was ruled by the Babylonians for a period of twenty years between 1830 and 1810 B.C., and thus it is not surprising to find complete apathy about music. For example, Ashurnasirpal III, who reigned from 883 to 859 B.C., spent his leisure time designing battering rams instead of composing operas and sonatas for unaccompanied banjo. It is true that he did decorate his palace with bas-reliefs, but these have no resem-

---

[1] Horace Walpole, *Geschichte der verdammten babylonischen Musik*, vol. 375, p. 4,867. See also Beethoven (Hermann), but note that his scholarship is full of potholes.

blance to our modern bass fiddle as some historians contend.[2] Furthermore, Rembrandt's famous portrait of Ashurnasirpal III reveals a man who is cruelty personified, despite the hypocritical attempt to veil this cruelty by his affectation of feminine curls. It is best to move on again.

Phoenician Music

The Phoenician alphabet consisted of twenty-two consonants and no vowels which made it somewhat difficult for Phoenician singers to hold their mouths open.

Persian Music

The great Greek historian, Herodotus, wrote at great length about Persia. It seems best to move on.

Egyptian Music

The Egyptians stole their music from Asia Minor, and for this reason we can move along very shortly to Greece.[3] Musical scholars do know, however, that Hatshepsut was the wife of Thutmose II, and that she soon became the wife of Thutmose III.[4] And Hatshepsut died in 1,480 B.C., but as David Crockett's famous painting of Hatshepsut reveals, she was certainly

[2] Grosswetter and Pickelsnart, obviously.

[3] Dr. Steinglissinger's nephew Dr. Ludwig Hans Stoneslider summed up the situation in his *History of Egyptian Music*, vol. 356, p. 5,329: "These are the times that try men's souls."

[4] She at least waited until Thutmose II had been embalmed.

not the kind of woman to be interested in string quartets, or even football band marches.[5]

Professor Heissfuss also pointed out that Hatshepsut was also known as Hatshepset and Hatasu, and that Thutmose was sometimes known as Thothmes. Whether this indicates dishonesty on their part or a lack of elementary education in spelling in Egypt, it seems advisable to move on to Greece where things will improve.

> *As we have seen, there is little cheer for the music historian in Babylonia and Egypt, but significant scholars remember Lohengrin Schniffelbauch's courageous words: "Brave admiral, say but one good word. What shall we do when hope is gone? The words leapt like a leaping sword: 'Sail on! Sail on! and on!'"*

[5] Edelweiss Bentschlagen, the Director of Football Bands at the University of Schwarznagel an der Ruhr, disagrees in his *Geschichte des Fussball*, but as Hugo Heissfuss pointed out, Bentschlagen does not know a Dudelsack from a Krummbogen. This, of course, leads one to suspect his scholarship.

7

GREECE

he organ fugues of Hermann von Süssen-pfeiffer and the string quartets of Bridgette Hissenbaum are not too far in the future when the musical scholar reaches Greece.[1] And, perhaps, for this reason we should move on immediately. However, significant musical developments occurred here, particularly on the island of Crete.

Cretan Music

Tessie Burnheart's explorations in Crete during the winter of 1838 opened up an entirely new field of music research. Fortunately, the present writer carried on in this significant field and thus those who have purchased his treatise *From* Pithecanthropus erectus *to King Minos* have enjoyed the unique opportunity to make a detailed study of the beginnings of Greek music.[2]

[1] On the title page of her monumental *Die griechische Musikinstru-mente und Musiknoten*, Miss Burnheart wrote the following famous words: "Oh, frabjous day! Callooh! Callay! He chortled in his joy."

[2] This work may be obtained by writing immediately to the present writer with an enclosure of $89.27. No trading stamps, please.

As musical scholars know, the Cretans [3] utilized bronze as far back as 4,001 B.C., and as one would surmise, all of their music was scored for the bronze-bone flute (ulnas and clavicles, for the most part, although one bronze jaw-bone flute has been found) instead of for the antiquated bone flute (femurs and radiuses, mostly), and as we have noted, the latter tended to overblow at the minor second.[4]

The bronze-bone flute, on the other hand, would not blow at all. One of these (an ulna) is shown below.

We do know, however, that the majority of Cretan compositions were sung by the women and not by the men, since the chests of the former were wonderfully developed. This is revealed in Gainsborough's popular portrait of Ios, Crete's most famous female singer.

---

[3] Doctoral candidates should be cautioned that Cretans are not necessarily cretins despite the inference in Wolfgang Offenschmiezel's notorious work.

[4] Which is not always desirable.

An examination of this portrait indicates clearly that the Italian *bel canto* tradition began in Crete, and not in Italy.[5]

Unfortunately, Ios and the marvelously developed *bel canto* chests disappeared in 1,400 B.C. when King Minos's palace of Cnossus was destroyed (by the volume of Ios's voice, it is said). For this reason, we must move on to Greece proper. Or as Dr. Steinglissinger wrote: "*Lass uns nach Griechenland gehen. Der griechische Busen ist wunderbar!*" [6]

Greece Proper

Discussions of Greek music normally begin with Homer, but there is an increasing tendency on the part of scholars to be somewhat suspicious of this man.[7] At one time he loomed solidly upon the historical horizon as the undisputed author of the *Iliad* and *Odyssey*, both of which he wrote in July of 802 B.C.[8] But now we are not quite so sure that he *was* the author of these two best-sellers. Doubts are even being cast upon the suggestion that Homer ever wrote anything. But the most serious part of the matter is that we are not even certain that Homer was ever Homer.

Now it should be obvious that serious musical scholarship rests upon the bedrock of truth. Scholars must feel that the men

---

[5] As might be expected, Miss Burnheart's discovery of this tradition was met by strong opposition on the part of the Italian music historian, Dr. Pietro Antonio Zucchini, in his *Storia della arte Cretanini*, vol. 76, p. 2,345, where Dr. Zucchini wrote: "*Per favore, potrebe dirigermi al babinetto.*" In the English edition this has been rather freely translated as: "O villain, villain, smiling, damned villain!"

[6] Hugo Steinglissinger, *Studien über griechische Busen*, vol. 7,429, p. 25,438. Dr. Steinglissinger's young brother Dr. Horatio Stoneslider pointed out in his translation of this work (*Studies on Greek Bosoms*) that his older brother's final sentence quoted above has been misinterpreted by some poorly educated historians. As Dr. Stoneslider wrote, the correct translation is: "Let us to Greece go. The Greek bosom is wonderful!"

[7] The fact that Homer did not possess a first name should have made some men question his integrity.

[8] July 4 through 7 according to Disselhoffer.

and women about which they write are honest. They are perfectly willing and even eager to discuss a Homer or a Beethoven, but to wake up some morning only to learn that neither man ever lived makes it difficult to write about the *Iliad* or the *Eroica Symphony* with a great deal of enthusiasm. Fortunately for historians, most great men and women are reputable, but it is apparent that Homer was not one of these. For this reason we move on to Greeks of integrity.

There is no reason for the scholar to be suspicious of Sappho's moral fibre.[9] Born on October 3, 601 B.C., Sappho had three brothers known as Larichus, Charaxus, and Anonymous.[10] Her mother's name was Cleïs.[11] We know that Charaxus was involved with a young courtesan, Doricha, known as Rhodopis.[12]

Sappho is of particular importance to the music historian because she invented the female conservatory of music that has lasted to this day in some cities. We know very little about her curriculum, but we do know that her conservatory went bankrupt, since, sad to say, an extant drawing shows her, shoes in hands, sneaking away from her creditors. (See next page.) It is apparent that we must move on to more reliable people.

At one time music historians devoted a great deal of space to Sappho's Uncle Chiron, but since the discovery of Botticelli's painting of Chiron and his wife, Anaxtoria, most scholars have doubted Chiron's role in the development of the baseball band

[9] See Pedro Dittersdorf's *Studien über Sappho Scamandronymus*, vol. 769, ·p. 2,594, where he quotes one of her poems as follows: "*Ich bin nicht gefärlich.*" This, of course, may be translated as, "O, my offense is rank, it smells to heaven."

[10] As Dr. Antonio Buffo pointed out, Anonymous was a very common name in Lesbos.

[11] We think that Cleïs was her mother, but as Sappho, herself, wrote in her famous poem, "To Mother", "What's in a name? That which we call a rose by any other name would smell as sweet."

[12] This is the only possible suggestion of dishonesty connected with Sappho, since if Doricha moved under cover of an assumed name or alias, the fact throws some doubt upon the reputation of the entire family. On the other hand, we must remember what Charaxus said: "My sister! my sweet sister! if a name dearer and purer were, it should be thine."

march. He appears to be the sort of uncle that one would not trust with a favorite niece, if one is to judge by his shifty eyes.

We therefore move on to Hipponax.[13] It was he that said, "Lay on, Macduff, and damn'd be him that first cries 'Hold, enough!'" For this reason, we shall move on to the more gentle Anacreon who was born in 563 B.C.

Anacreon is of immense importance to the history of music because he was the first of a long line of child prodigies to be taken on concert tours by their parents. Anacreon[14] was only three when he began to compose simple but fresh little songs with lyre accompaniments, and his parents realized that he was a child prodigy. It is fortunate for posterity that Dr. Sophie Hightower discovered Anacreon's first little song, the words of which may be translated as follows:

O fairy foot! O shapely leg! O tempting taper thigh!
O comely back! O clipsome waist! with ivory which vie;
O shoulders soft! O budding breasts! O neck of swan-like fall!
O lovely hands! O lustrous eyes! for which I madden all.

Although no knowledgeable person would expect more of even a three-year-old prodigy, there is in the above song a growing note of maturity that Anacreon's father, Perseus, realized must be nourished. As Renoir's famous drawing on the next page indicates, Anacreon was placed on his father's knee where he might gain a better understanding of life firsthand. In the meanwhile, the young child studied hard, and when he was eight his parents felt that he was ready for his first tour as a child prodigy.

Starting at Corinth, Anacreon performed a program of his songs with lyre accompaniment to a full house in the open-air theater on the outskirts of the city. He was immediately hailed as a child prodigy on the lyre, and as a song writer of great promise. The critics particularly applauded his latest composition that ended with the following lines.

While, greedily, Rose drew me to her kiss,
More rare with Susan was my stolen bliss.

[13] His last name was Thorax.
[14] His last name was Necropolis.

It was apparent that Anacreon's talks with his father on the latter's knee were bearing fruit, and he was booked into all of the musical centers throughout the mainland and on the islands. But by the time Anacreon was ten years of age something happened. Due to Dr. Hightower's extensive research we now know what happened: Anacreon burned himself out with his poetry, and died with Rose and Susan in his arms. For this reason, we must move on.[15]

The last honest Greek was Pythagoras, whose integrity has never been doubted.[16] Although he was not known as a composer, Pythagoras was extremely important for his investigations in the field of acoustics. He discovered that if one tuned a one-string violin to middle C, and then sawed the violin in half, each half would produce a C one octave higher than the original. This is demonstrated as follows:

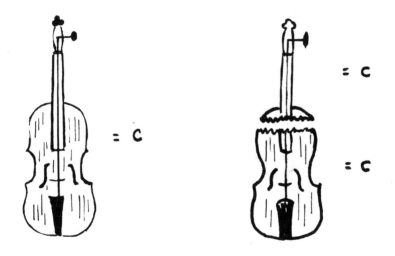

---

[15] Dr. Hightower quotes Anacreon's last words: "And that dismal cry arose slowly and sank slowly through the air, 'Pan is dead!—Great Pan is dead—Pan, Pan is dead.'"

[16] His first name was Joseph, although his close friends called him Joe.

Pythagoras carried this vital experiment even further and soon found that if one saws a violin into three segments, each of the resulting parts produces a G above the original C. He continued this investigation for a period of twenty-two years,[17] and the results are known to every school boy:

> *Theorem XXII.* If one continues to saw a violin into parts, one soon ends up with no violin.

Now, as every musical scholar realizes, this theorem led to the invention of the piano which is difficult to saw into parts. But we must wait some time before this occurs.

Two other things may or may not have had an effect on the development of the football band and the string quartet. Pythagorus and his followers would not eat beans.[18] Furthermore, he was a coward when it came to entering cold water for his morning swim, as the famous portrait shows.

[17] Until February 23, 587 B.C., according to Benjamin Franklin's careful calculations. This has been disputed by Handel (Adolf), but this need not disturb us.

[18] Pythagoras's well-known poem on this subject ends as follows: "O thou weed, who art so lovely fair and smell'st so sweet that the senses ache at thee, would thou hadst ne'er been born."

Although musical scholars have been searching for many years, it seems impossible to find another honest Greek composer—or one who does not burn himself out with his poetry by the age of ten. And it is just as difficult to find architects or sculptors of integrity, since as this writer has pointed out,[19] the Parthenon would be preserved intact if the two architects (Ictinus and Callicrates) had not been dishonest when mixing cement with gravel and sand.[20] And it is well known that Greek sculptors cheated their patrons by producing unfinished statues without arms.[21] Furthermore, costs were cut by eliminating the statues' clothes.[22]

For all of these reasons, therefore, it seems best to move on to Rome when moral fibres will be stronger.[23]

> *The great Chinese musical scholar, Professor Sing wen Low, is the acknowledged world authority on Greek music, but even he became sick and tired of it as one can see in his oft-quoted essay* Moral Turpitude in Lesbian Music: "*My heart aches, and a drowsy numbness pains my sense, as though of hemlock I had drunk with beaded bubbles winking at the brim, and purple-stained mouth.*"

[19] In his treatise, *From* Pithecanthropus erectus *to* Picasso, p. 76,293.

[20] See Otto Grosskopf's *Studien über Portland Cement*, vol. 537, p. 6,395.

[21] Braunschweiger devised a theory that the sculptors saved money by hiring as models slaves whose arms had been removed for minor traffic violations. However, this seems unlikely, since as Dr. Grosskopf has proved, slaves were not allowed to drive in Greece.

[22] See Gertrude Schwissenhip's *Studien über die Nacktheit*, vol. 347, p. 2,789, where she wrote: "*Hoch der Nacktheit!*" In her own translation of this work (*Studies on Nakedness*), she wrote: "Life is made up of sobs, sniffles, and smiles, with sniffles predominating."

[23] Julius Caesar's well-known poem, however, fills us with forebodings:

> *There was a little girl*
> *Who had a little curl*
> *Right in the middle of her forehead,*
> *And when she was good*
> *She was very, very good,*
> *And when she was bad she was horrid.*

8

ROME

ooks on the history of music seldom devote more than a page or two to Roman music, the only exception being Pedro Albuquerque's masterful sixty-four volume edition.[1] The main difficulty confronting us is the fact that we have no Roman music to discuss.

We do, however, encounter the second child prodigy in history to be taken on concert tours by his parents. Petronius Catullus was born on March 4, 87 B.C.[2] He showed an early spark and began to compose simple songs to the accompaniment of the tuba when he was but two years of age. His father[3] and mother[4] recognized immediately that their young son was a genius, and arranged to give him lessons on the tuba.

The young Catullus progressed rapidly and at the age of two and one-half, his first published song appeared. As the following excerpt reveals, it is a simple and tender little song as befitting

[1] Pedro Albuquerque, *Historia musica de Roma.*

[2] It may be of considerable interest to know that this writer was also born on March 4, although not in 87 B.C, as some of his students have suggested.

[3] Gaius

[4] Brixia

his tender years, and yet one can see that the child is slowly beginning to mature.[5]

> *Acme, as her lover said,*
> *Lightly bending back her head,*
> *And with lips of ruby skimming*
> *His tipsy eyes, in pleasure swimming;*
> *"Septimillus! darling mine,*
> *So may we thus ever twine."*

By the time young Catullus was six, his parents took him on his first concert tour of the provinces, and his success was immediate. For three years he traveled and sang his simple songs to the accompaniment of the tuba, but something happened. We might just as well admit it: nine-year-old Petronius Catullus had burned himself out. He could no longer maintain the pace of writing daily about Acme and Lesbia. He did try Lydia—"Lydia! girl of prettiest mien, and fairest skin, that e'er were seen."—but it was no use. He was through, or as Dr. Ole Heisslippen wrote, *"Er war kaputt!"*[6] There is no denying the fact that Brutus Caligula's famous portrait of Catullus and Acme reveals the reason why.

[5] From Kurt Hissenbach's *Studien über Acme*. The translation is by his father, Dr. Johannes Hissenbach, in the American edition, *Studies on Acme*. Doctoral candidates in music should be warned, however, that the pictures in the English edition have been expurgated so that younger music students will not be led away from their exercises and scales.

[6] Ole Heisslippen, *Studien über Lesbia*, vol. 792, p. 5,249. As Dr. Heisslippen said: "The memory of the just is blessed; but the name of the wicked shall rot."

For this reason we move on to Gaius Suetonius, the great Roman music historian, whose significant work, *Lives of the Twelve Caesars*, gives us a remarkable picture of musical life in Imperial Rome. One salient fact appears: Nero's favorite singer, Menecrates, sang in the bathtub, although Suetonius fails to say whether Nero did this also. We must, however, assume that he did. Nero was that type of person.

One other major treatise concerning Roman music has come down to us, the *Golden Ass* of Lucius Apuleius. But as El Greco's famous portrait of Apuleius reveals, his clarinet was split down the middle and would not have played well. Furthermore, Apuleius's hands were too large for a clarinet.

It is obvious, therefore, that there is little in Rome for the intellectually curious scholar, and for this reason we must move on to the Dark Ages when children do not wear themselves out with their poetry, and when there is more interest in developing basketball bands, accordion ensembles, and string quartets.

Pedro Prendergast's summary of Roman music is familiar to all significant musical scholars. An intensely moral man, Professor Prendergast could only say: "My Hypsithilla, charming fair, my life, my soul, ah, hear my prayer. Prepare thy bosom to receive all that so much love can give."

9

THE
DARK AGES

ome modern historians remind us constantly that the Dark Ages were not dark at all, but scholarly music historians are not swayed by hasty pronouncements. There is no escaping the fact that Dr. Pufendorf's gargantuan investigation into the period following the Fall of Rome on January 2, A.D. 476 [1] reveals absolutely nothing but darkness. But as he wrote in his monumental treatise on this subject, "*C'est la guerre!*" [2]

Nevertheless, two rather bright spots appear during the Dark Ages. The first is in Bulgaria where a whole series of enlightened rulers encouraged musical composition and still found time for their mistresses.[3] The most important of these rulers were Kurt

[1] At 5:43 P.M. See Pompejus Pufendorf's *Studien über* A.D. *476*, vol. 358, p. 43,579, for the evidence. Music scholars may note also that it was raining at that time.

[2] This, of course, appears in the *Histoire de la Rome* which is the French translation of Dr. Alburqueque's *Historia musica de Roma*, cited above somewhere. In the English translation by his godson, Aldrich Alburqueque, the above remark appears as, "Life ain't all beer and skittles!"

[3] Boris Godunov, *Geschichte der bulgarischen Musik*, vol. 35, p. 2,849.

I (484–526), Anonymous I (642–643), Tervel XVI (701–718), Anonymous II (718–724), Kormisosh XXII (739–756), Telets IV (761–764), Sabin I (764), Pagin I (764–766),[4] Umor X (766), Tokt I (766–768),[5] Anonymous III (777–791), and Anonymous IV (792–800).[6] Some college music appreciation books speak also of Krum VII (808–814), but he was not well bred and thus should be avoided.

[4] Sabin and Pagin were half-brothers, but Sabin was throttled by Pagin and so did not reign long.

[5] Umor and Tokt were also half-brothers.

[6] Who escaped from Bulgaria in 800 and became Charlemagne in France—or Karl der Grosse in Germany—depending upon which country you come from.

It is the reign of Anonymous II that is of special interest to us, since the string quartet was nearly invented at this time. Unfortunately, there were no violins, violas, or cellos in Bulgaria at this time. Inasmuch as violins, violas, and cellos had not been invented yet, history should not continue to condemn the Bulgarians. Their music was, therefore, written for two treble bullroarers, one tenor bullroarer, and one bass bullroarer, but since the treble bullroarer produces a tone similar to the Peruvian whistling pot, we may move on to the Court of Charlemagne which is the other bright spot in the Dark Ages.

As serious musical scholars know, Charlemagne was married four times and had six mistresses. For this reason he had very little time for music.[7] Or for his wife, as Alcuin's famous portrait on page 45 reveals.

This leads us to the Middle Ages when things will improve immeasurably.

Hans Gassenpumpf was the first to direct scholars' attention to Charlemagne's influence on the development of music: "Sits he on never so high a throne, a man still sits on his bottom."

[7] The names of his wives were: Hedwig, Liese, Amalia, and Emma. The names of his mistresses were: Rose, Mathilde, Lucie, Annchen, Else, and Wilhelmine. For the names of his children, see Dr. Oswald Tortilla's *Studien über die Kinder von Karl dem Grossen,* vol 852, pp. 486–902. The young music graduate student should be warned, however, that Dr. Tortilla admitted that his list is not complete. As he said, "Were it not for imagination, a man would be as happy in the arms of a chambermaid as of a Duchess."

10

THE
MIDDLE AGES

hen we enter the Middle Ages, that is, from the years 1,000 to 1,300,[1] we encounter the first truly significant developments in musical culture during the Paleolithic era. We note immediately that nearly everyone likes music, even in countries other than Bulgaria. And although women were not allowed to sing during the Dark Ages, we find them joyful and vocal once again. This is illustrated clearly in the oft-quoted poem by the famous composer, Guido Cavalcanti who lived in the early thirteenth century.[2]

> *Her naked feet still had the dews on them,*
> *As, singing like a lover, so she came;*
> *Joyful, and fashioned for all ecstasy.*

Thanks to Dr. Yamagata, we have the original painting of her naked feet. Note that the ravages of time have erased much of the

---

[1] See Ito Yamagata's *Geschichte der Musik des Mittelalters,* vol. 546, p. 7,392, where he established the fact that the Middle Ages began on January 2 (4:44 A.M.) and ended on December 30 (11:53 P.M.).

[2] And burned himself out at the age of seven.

dew, but fortunately, much of the painting has been preserved.

It is such things as this that make the musical scholar happy to do research in the Middle Ages. It is all very well to insist that the Dark Ages were not dark, but they are extremely dull to the scholar with red blood coursing through his veins. Very few naked feet had dew on them between the Fall of Rome and January 2 (4:44 A.M.), A.D. 1000.[3]

Unfortunately, the music that was sung by the young lady has been lost, but scholars have not lost all hope. Serious music scholars *never* lose hope. This is the history of music history: endless toil; never-ending research in damp, musty libraries, museums, and monasteries; ceaseless perusal of torn manuscripts; tear-stained pages from lovers' diaries; hours, days, weeks, months, years spent in the unending search for a fragment of historical truth; hope never diminishing in the everlasting search for something as beautiful as:

Her naked feet still had the dews on them . . .

So our scholarly investigations continue. And in the southern part of England we encounter the third child prodigy of our his-

---

[3] This subject is discussed at length by Dr. Yamagata's youngest grandson, Dr. Otto Putsch, whose treatise, *The History of Naked Feet*, contains the rest of this poem as follows: "Blessings on thee, little man, barefoot boy, with cheek of tan."

torical study. Harold Albert Hightower was born August 15, 1278, of humble parents who lived in a modest frame house in Wither-on-the-Vine, Lower Sussex—on Hastings Street.[4] He began to compose simple, fresh little songs when he was but twenty-seven, and as his parents realized that he was a child prodigy, they arranged to give him lessons on the clarinet.

Unfortunately, Harold discovered that the clarinet would not be invented for about four hundred years, so he decided to study the Welsh crwth instead.[5] The young man progressed rapidly in his musical studies and by the time he had reached the age of thirty-seven, his father and mother arranged for his first concert tour. He toured for fifty years as a distinguished crwthist, but Harold never achieved the promised success as a writer of songs. Professor Gretchen Spruchdichter's research revealed the reason why. Harold never learned to spell, as the following lines from one of his obscure songs reveal.

Sumer is icumen in lhude sing cucu.
Groweth sed and bloweth med and springth the wode nu.

This leads us inevitably to the Renaissance when children have an opportunity to learn spelling and grammar.[6]

Harold Hightower's noted biographer, Ivanovitch Weedov, could see no reason for leaving the Middle Ages and the naked feet with dews on them: "Dally not with my desire, nor quash with thy delays my fire. Bursting with love upon my couch I lie, forestalling with desire the distant joy."

[4] In the 2700 block on the east side of the street.
[5] This, of course, illustrates the strong influence wielded by the Phoenician vowel-less alphabet on Wales.
[6] Dr. Spruchdichter refers to this in her treatise *The History of Shame* when she writes, "There smites nothing so sharp, nor smelleth so sour as shame."

11

THE RENAISSANCE

ost music historians begin their books with the Renaissance. It is a period of great activity and promise. Books begin to be written in English, French, German, Italian, and Danish, and thus are easier to understand. Books contain more pictures and thus are more enjoyable to look at. Women wear lower necklines and thus are more interesting to contemplate.

The Renaissance is, in truth, a period of great activity. Great painters, great poets, great sculptors, great architects, great dramatists, great composers—all now appear and create the greatest paintings, the greatest poetry, the greatest statues, the greatest buildings, the greatest plays, and the greatest musical compositions of all time.

There is no denying it. The normal music scholar simply cannot wait until he can discuss the Renaissance. The roots of the string quartet, symphony, concerto, opera, sonata, and football band march are all there to lead us onward to Gottfried von Hohenlaufen, Johann Christoph Schmiezel, Putnam Basil Trowbridge and, of course, Bridgette Hissenbaum.

The difficulty is to demonstrate a truly scholarly restraint in the face of these riches. Only the mature music historian should attempt to do research in this period; younger men would be wise to do their initial investigations in less exotic eras. Promising young scholars have been warped for life and ruined by sudden encounters with Petrarch, Laura, Beatrice, Machaut, Rabelais, Boccaccio, and Violetta. But with proper guidance, this shock could have been softened, and this is what the present writer wishes to do at this time. Each of the great composers of this age will be discussed soberly and their frailties will be treated with scholarly circumspection. Pictures will be kept to a bare minimum. A great number of long footnotes will be appended for sobering purposes.[1]

The first great composer of the Renaissance—and there are scholars who rate him far above Bach,[2] Beethoven,[3] Brahms,[4] Bartok,[5] and Schmidt[6]—is Guillaume de Machaut who was born on January 1, 1300, and began to compose complex works immediately. His first composition, the *Sonata No. 1 for Unaccompanied Krummhorn*, Op. 1, No. 1,[7] was completed on his first birthday, and this was quickly followed by his well-known *Trio for Two Rebecs and Trumscheit*, Op. 1, No. 2.

These early compositions led his mother[8] and father[9] to suspect that the young child might have a musical future before him, and he was enrolled immediately in the Conservatoire de Rheims where he studied portative organ under Jacques de Chan-

---

[1] This entire matter is discussed at considerable length by Dr. Pierre Fragonard in his well-known *Histoire de la nudité*, vol. 538, pp. 9,862–10,994. This is, of course, the book that German publishers refused to print. But as Dr. Steinglissinger's grandnephew Dr. Albert Stoneslider said, "It's better to wear out than rust out."

[2] Otto.

[3] Friedrich.

[4] Marguerite.

[5] Peter.

[6] Heinrich.

[7] "Op." is the abbreviation of the name of the man who arranged Machaut's works in chronological order for posterity. This man, Opie Dartmore, is very reliable.

[8] Olga.

[9] Pierre.

tilly and canon and fugue under Jean de Paris, both reliable men, and well liked by students and faculty alike. Young Guillaume's progress was remarkable and he graduated from the Conservatoire in 1305 with a Diploma in Canon and Fugue which entitled him to affix the honored letters, D.C.F., to his signature.[10] His graduation portrait, painted by El Greco, still hangs in the Louvre.

Unfortunately, Machaut had nearly burned himself out at the Conservatoire and publishers began to drop his music from their lists. He had accepted the position of organist at a small church

[10] He did not sign his name very often, however, since his only education was in portative organ and canon and fugue, and he never learned to spell well. In fact, he never could decide upon the way to sign his own name, and we find it as "Machault," "Mashow," "Macheaux," "Mascholdt," and "Mahshow," among others. This has led to some confusion.

on the left bank of the Seine and he continued to perform there for fifty-five years. By that time, his name had sunk into oblivion. And on top of this he got the gout and lost the sight of one eye.

On his sixtieth birthday, however, Guillaume de Machaut met Peronelle d'Armentieres, and it is from this day that he began to write those songs that we perform in our living rooms even to this day. Peronelle was young and inspirational and one of Machaut's last songs, "*Douce dame jolie*" (which must be translated as "Deuce, Jolly Dame"), was written especially for her.

It is our good fortune that Machaut had his portrait painted after his meeting with Peronelle, and preserved his happiness for posterity to perceive. It is unfortunate that no likeness of Peronelle exists, but her husband would not allow her to pose.

We do, however, have a drawing of Machaut's bed.[11] (See next page.)

[11] This is, of course, from Dr. Knut Olsen's famous treatise, *Studien über Machauts Bett*, vol. 642, p. 9,437. Dr. Olsen apologizes for this drawing, but as he points out, Machaut's original bed was destroyed the night of October 3, 1376, when his house was burned by Peronelle's husband. Dr. Olsen nevertheless states that this drawing is a reasonable and reliable facsimile. As he wrote in the Preface of his treatise (the translation into English is his own), "Early to bed and early to rise, makes a man healthy, wealthy, and wise."

There were notable composers in Italy also, among which we
must note Jacopo da Balogna (the inventor of Bologna Sausage
in 1343),[12] and Ghirardello da Firenze (the inventor of Ghirardello Chocolate in 1346).[13] Bartolomeo da Bologna also did some
serious composing but spent most of his time in his brother's
sausage factory. We find a great deal of their music in the
Squarcialupi Codex, but this firm went out of business in 1397
and consequently all fourteenth-century Italian music is now out
of print.[14]

For this reason it is fortunate that we can move on to Dijon
in Burgundy which became the center of musical composition
during the first half of the fifteenth century. The Duke of Burgundy, Charles the Bold, was particularly enthusiastic about orchestral music, and his Dijon Women's Symphony Orchestra

[12] See Aubrey O'Flaherty's *Geschichte der Wurst.*
[13] See Giovanni Spizza's *Geschichte der Kakao.*
[14] Or as Dr. Agnes Watenabe said, "*Gut!*"

became famous throughout Western Europe.[15] Fra Angelico's

[15] The personnel of the orchestra was as follows: conductor, Sylvie; first rebecs, Henriette (concert mistress), Agnes, Paule, and Rose-Marie; second rebecs, Gertrude, Irene, Dorothee, and Claire; tenor fiddles, Isabelle and Josephine; bass vielles, Alice and Edith; buisine, Rosalie; musette, Constance; flaustes traversaines, Laure and Judith; grosse hersumper, Emma. As Igor Pskov pointed out, Charles the Bold sometimes played with the women too.

popular painting of the orchestra during an intermission clearly indicates the reason for the Duke's enthusiasm. Charles the Bold also commissioned a great number of compositions from leading Burgundian women composers, but they seldom found time to write music due to their other duties at the Duke's court.[16]

As he grew older and weaker, Charles the Bold became less interested in female orchestras but he developed a taste for chamber music and this provided considerable employment for his famed Dijon Women's String Quartet.[17] As Charles grew even older and weaker, he lost his taste for everything except unaccompanied sonatas on the grosse hersumper.[18] We must move on.

During the last half of the fifteenth century we encounter several other composers, notably Josquin Deprez, Johannes Ockeghem, and Jacob Obrecht, but they need not detain us long. As usual, integrity is lacking, since Ockeghem also traveled under the names Jean or Jan, while Deprez's conduct was scandalous: during the first part of his life he used the alternate name Des Pres; during his last years he attempted to hide his past by the alias, Josee van der Weyden. It is quite obvious that such impostors are not going to contribute to the development of the string quartet or grass hockey band—and so Bridgette Hissenbaum remains in the far future. For this reason, we must move on again.

Unfortunately no honest composers are encountered until we reach Palestrina and Lassus, both of whom died in 1594 [19] after writing a great amount of music for *a capella* choirs—groups that cannot afford to hire piano or orchestral accompaniments. Again, however, the scholar is beset by rank dishonesty. Lassus hid behind two aliases: Orlando di Lasso and Roland de Lassus. And Palestrina was even more deceitful: his real name was Giovanni Pierluigi. Furthermore, his parents had him welded per-

[16] Dusting, scrubbing, cooking, and washing. Pfissenhorst disagrees, but his morals are suspect.

[17] Mathilde (first rebec), Louise (second rebec), Rosalie (tenor fiddle), and Christine (bass trumscheidt).

[18] Played by Liese Grossenwort.

[19] They killed each other in a duel.

manently inside a suit of armor so that he would not bother the female singers in his choir. Vermeer's well-known portrait of

him reveals the sad case. There is certainly no reason for music scholars to linger here, since if Richard Wagner had been forced to depend upon these two scoundrels, he never would have composed his many string quartets and marches for pilgrims.

As Dr. Juan López has shown, England produced no music of any kind during the Renaissance.[20]

And there were only a few developments in the United States and Canada at this time, although the *Suite in C* by the young Algonquin composer, Hiawatha, retained its popularity for some time.[21] For this reason, we may move on to the Baroque period which will offer untold riches.

The most scholarly summary of musical developments during the Renaissance was formulated by Sir Cedric O'Hooligan, Professor of Music at Tweedingsham University on the Thames: "Upon the smoothly shaven lawn, beneath the skies of May, oh, boys and girls, this merry morn, come out and play croquet."

[20] See Juan Gonzales López, *Studien über Heinrich VIII*, vol. 734, p. 2,369.

[21] This was written for five thigh bones of Potawatomi and will be discussed later in considerable detail.

12

THE
BAROQUE

n January 1, 1600, all of the Renaissance composers died and we find ourselves in a new era that encouraged the type of music that leads to Bridgette Hissenbaum. Opera was invented.[1] Oratorio was invented.[2] And it will not be long before fugues, canons, concertos, cantatas, suites, chorales, trio sonatas, and marches for badminton bands will be invented also in order that Gottfried von Hohenlaufen, Johann Christophe Schmiezel, Putnam Basil Trowbridge and, of course, Bridgette Hissenbaum can compose that music treasured by all of us.

We turn first to the invention of opera. History tells us that certain men gathered at the modest home of Count Bardi[3] in Florence and read Plato to each other.[4] They also took turns reading Aeschylus, Sophocles, Euripides, and Aesop.[5] They dis-

---

[1] January 1 at 6:31 A.M.
[2] January 2 at 11:37 P.M.
[3] As Dr. Andrew Jackson pointed out in his famous *Studien über Jazz*, Count Basie was *not* in Florence at that time regardless of Pfissenhauser's statement.
[4] On alternate Thursday evenings.
[5] On alternate Monday evenings.

covered that the ancient Greeks had already invented opera, but since no one else knew this, they decided to write their own operas.[6]

They were fortunate to have some of Florence's most illustrious musicians in their midst: Ottavio Rinuccini,[7] Vincenzo Galilei,[8] Giulio Caccini, and Peri.[9] Their first opera was called *Dafne*, the Italian misspelling of Daphnis. Then Peri and Caccini wrote *Euridice*. As a matter of fact, they wrote two Euridices.[10]

These operas met with immediate success because they enabled wealthy women to wear evening gowns to opening nights. They also enabled singers to sing louder than they could in preceding historical periods. For this reason we move on to Claudio Monteverdi who composed the first operatic masterpiece—his famous *Orfeo* [11]—in 1607.

This opera has not only endured throughout the ages, but it utilized the new recitative style, a type of nonmusical song that opera composers use for conversations which should remain spoken dialogue. An example of this from *Orfeo* is as follows: [12]

> ORPHEUS: "Euridice?"
> EURIDICE: *(No answer)*
> ORPHEUS: "Euridice?" *(Louder)*
> EURIDICE: *(No answer)*
> ORPHEUS: "Euridice!" *(Much Louder)*
> EURIDICE: "Who is calling?" *(From afar)*
> ORPHEUS: "Me. Orpheus."
> EURIDICE: *(Drawing nearer)* "Who?"
> ORPHEUS: "Oh, hell!"

[6] They were sick and tired of listening to Palestrina's music.

[7] Who really was not a musician at all, but was just a mediocre poet.

[8] Father of Galileo Galilei, whom we address by the first name.

[9] His father and mother never gave him a first name.

[10] One would have been more than enough.

[11] The Italian misspelling of Orpheus, the hero of an extremely melancholy story.

[12] The music of this section has been lost, and no one has bothered to look for it.

After Monteverdi died in 1643, a great number of operas were written in Italy, but they need not detain us here. The only development that may be of interest to the inquiring scholar is that as the number of operas increased, there was a concomitant demand for more singers with loud voices, and this demand was met.[13]

During this period, England was not interested in opera. However, when Henry Purcell was born in 1659 or thereabouts,[14] he displayed an early interest in composing small operatic scenes, one of which begins as follows.

> *Nay, pish; nay; phew! nay, faith and will you? Fie!*
> *A gentleman and use me thus! I'll cry.*

When his parents saw this, they realized that he was a child prodigy and arranged to give him lessons in counterpoint, canon and fugue—and placed him immediately in a home for wayward children at Chelsea. Young Henry developed rapidly, and when he was only five years old he produced his famous opera *Dido and Aeneas* before an invited audience.[15] One of its recitatives, modeled after those by Monteverdi, is as follows.[16]

> DIDO: "Aeneas?"
> AENEAS: *(No answer)*
> DIDO: "Aeneas?" *(Louder)*
> AENEAS: *(No answer)*

[13] With the cooperation of Italian mothers and fathers.

[14] We are not sure because his father and mother were not sure.

[15] And guards. Purcell conducted this performance at the virginal with an orchestra made up of inmates from the Chelsea school: four viols, three zinks, seven lutes, five cromornes, ten trumscheits, fifteen vihuelas, twenty-four sackbuts, fifty-one shawms, seventy-three cornets, and one hundred fifty-seven recorders. We do not have the names of the orchestral players, but the part of Dido was sung by Agnes Hillsbottom and Aeneas was sung by Albert Herringbone, two of the older inmates. Neither achieved further fame due to the absence of a parole system in England at that time.

[16] The music of this section has been lost and no one has bothered to look for it.

DIDO:	"Aeneas! Are you there?" *(Much louder)*
AENEAS:	*(From afar)* "Who is calling?"
DIDO:	"I. Dido."
AENEAS:	*(Drawing nearer)* "Who?"
DIDO:	"Oh, hell!"

For this reason, *Dido and Aeneas* was not followed by other operas. We move, therefore, to Germany where significant things will occur.

In 1643, the year that Monteverdi wrote his last recitative, Gottfried von Hohenlaufen was born in Mannheim, Germany. This is a year to be treasured by all serious music historians because this young genius was to be the first person to start music on its inexorable way toward Bridgette Hissenbaum and Sir Edward Elgar.[17]

Gottfried was only one year old when his father, Karl Christoph Heinrich Gottlieb von Hohenlaufen, took one look at his young son. We are fortunate that Penrod Dagurre photographed the father at that time, the picture being appended below.

[17] One of whom will not be discussed in this book. As Dr. Steinglissinger's mother, Dr. Hilda Stoneslider, said in her own treatise: "Caesar had his Brutus; Charles the First, his Cromwell; and George the Third may profit by their example. If this be treason, make the most of it."

However, in order to earn sufficient money for retirement from the army, the father taught young Gottlieb how to play the trombone and then took his two-year-old son on tours of Western Europe and the United States. Sitting in his father's lap, Gottfried performed all of the well-known sonatas for unaccompanied trombone before royalty, persons of high station, and high persons. Unfortunately, the pace was too fast for the young lad and his lip gave out during a concert at Whiskey Creek, Idaho, and his father was forced to take him back home to Mannheim.

When young Gottfried arrived home, his father [18] taught him how to play the organ so that the two of them might take further tours of Western Europe and the United States. But this was not to be. The precocious young man was offered the post of organist and choirmaster at the famous St. Stephen Church in Hamburg, and as he was but four years of age, he was one of the youngest organists in Germany at that time.

While his father retired on his son's church salary, young Gottfried played the organ, directed the choir, and composed music. And it is to this music that serious music scholars turn their attention, for by the time he was nine, young Gottfried von Hohenlaufen had startled the world by inventing the fugue, the chorale, the concerto grosso, the keyboard and orchestral suite, the sonata for unaccompanied violin and cello, the toccata, the cantata, the oratorio, and the Mass. However, he did not invent the football band march.[19]

It was at this time that Gottfried was visited by a young man with the obscure name of Johann Sebastian Bach, whose father and mother were also named Bach. As we see on next page, the picture of this shy young man standing near the organ loft, listening to the famous organist play, must have touched the heartstrings of Gottfried von Hohenlaufen.

Shy young Johann Sebastian Bach stood entranced for many days listening to the famous organist perform such well-known

[18] Music scholars have never found his mother.
[19] The St. Stephen Church did not encourage athletics.

works as the *Wohltemperiertes Klavierding*,[20] the six *Brannte-weine Konzerte*,[21] the *Musikalische Ogre*, and, of course, the

world-famous oratorio, the *Messiah*.[22]

Young Bach loved these works and he hid each night[23] in Gottfried von Hohenlaufen's attic in order to copy them down for future reference.[24] Upon his return to Epsom, young Bach

---

[20] To translate this as the *Well-Tempered Clavier Thing* is, of course, ridiculous. Von Hohenlaufen wrote this great work for the nine-foot Steinway concert grand piano, just invented by Magnus Steinway, the Scottish inventor.

[21] These concertos were composed to accompany the brandy course at Frederick the Great's state dinners.

[22] Erroneously attributed to Von Hohenlaufen's pupil, Handel, who was dishonest enough to claim the work as his own.

[23] For three and one-half years.

[24] One look at his picture above will reveal the shifty look in his eyes.

performed these works on the pandora, the only instrument he knew,[25] and published them as his own. He soon could afford to marry his cousin, Maria Barbara, who died in 1720, leaving him seven children to support. The next year he married Anna Magdalena, and despite his other duties, Bach found time to father thirteen more children. But that was the end of Johann Sebastian Bach despite what he wrote in his autobiography, *Mein Leben und meine Irrtümer*.[26] This leads us, of course, to a more important man, Johann Christoph Schmiezel, the inventor of the clarinet.

It is lamentable that some music historians continue to treat this noble instrument as a late eighteenth-century invention, since Schmiezel not only perfected it in 1727, but he also composed three hundred fifty concertos for clarinet and orchestra, all of which deserve to be performed.

[25] The pandora was an instrument named after the famous Greek girl's box.

[26] In her translation of this work (*My Life and Errors*), Dr. Olga Hassenbisch quotes Bach as follows: "Though I look old yet I am strong and lusty, for in my youth I never did apply hot and rebellious liquors in my blood."

When young Schmiezel was five years old, his mother, Gretchen Schmiezel, took one look at him and realized that her son was a child prodigy.[27] She taught the youngster to play the oboe and took him on several world tours. At the end of the year (1684), young Schmiezel accepted a position as solo oboist with Count Brugelhorn's orchestra at Esch on the banks of the Alzette, and thus he became the youngest solo oboist in Western Europe.

However, the buzzing of the oboe's double reed soon became irritating to young Schmiezel's lips and he cast about for a method of playing the oboe with a single reed that would not buzz. He worked for thirty-eight years, trying out single reed after single reed on his oboe until he found one that would not buzz. This remarkable new instrument, the Oboe-With-a-Single Reed, was immediately named the *Hoboe-mit-eines-Rohrblatt*.[28] For simplicity's sake, it is usually written as *Hoboemiteinesrohrblatt*.[29]

Schmiezel's one hundred fifty concertos for the *Hoboemiteinesrohrblatt* are now available in an East German edition, and his *Konzert in C Dur für Hoboemiteinesrohrblatt und Orchester*, Op. 796, No. 5,384, is especially recommended for the many performers who are tired of Mozart's uninspired works for the instrument.

Schmiezel's death in 1735 leads us directly to his stepson, Georg Frideric Händel, whose spelling of his first name without an "e" illustrates vividly the educational standards in the Düsseldorf public schools at that time. When he was born, he wrote his last name as Händel, but when he moved to England he found that English typewriters do not have an "a" with an *umlaut* (¨), so he wrote his name as Handel, after a great deal of thought, so he said.[30]

---

[27] Music scholars have never found his father. Nor did his mother.
[28] Because Schmiezel could not speak English.
[29] This was changed to "clarinet" in the United States during World War I due to anti-German sentiment.
[30] As he wrote in his autobiography, "Once upon a midnight dreary, while I pondered, weak and weary."

When Handel was born in 1685, his mother and stepfather realized that he was not a child prodigy, and for this reason he was not allowed to study music. However, in his twenty-fourth year in Düsseldorf Public School No. 13, young Georg wrote a little song for his class in English composition. Its words are as follows.

I pelt thee with an apple, Fair! if true love stir in thee,
Receive it willingly, and yield thy maiden charms to me.

Now, if young Handel had stopped right there, he would not have been expelled from Düsseldorf Public School No. 13, but the real cause for his expulsion was the picture that he drew of the apple.

After being expelled from school, Handel went to England and studied music with Gottfried von Hohenlaufen, but as we have seen, Handel published Hohenlaufen's oratorio the *Messiah* as his own work, and the rest is history. Handel was sent in a boatload of common thieves to New England where he died in 1759 imprisoned in the stocks still claiming the oratorio as his own.[31] Benjamin West's etching of the old thief reveals clearly the truth of the matter. We must now leave this pitiable story of

willful deceit and move on to the Classic Period of music when composers will be men of integrity.

Extremely few scholars have felt equal to the task of summarizing this most significant period of music, the great age of Gottfried von Hohenlaufen, Johann Christophe Schmiezel, and the latter's mother, Gretchen. Perhaps Gertrude Glowworm epitomized it the best when she wrote: "Oh! light of my life, I die within thine arms. Mine eyes are lost in vacancy. My head swims, my lips grow cold, ah! what is this strange quivering?"

[31] In his autobiography, *The Martyrdom of Georg F. Handel*, published by the Harvard College Press, Handel wrote with bitterness about humanity, and ended his essay with the following misanthropic theme: "Old dog Tray's ever faithful, grief cannot drive him away; he's gentle, he is kind; I'll never, never find a better friend than old dog Tray."

13

CLASSIC
MUSIC

 n their never-ending search for integrity, music scholars greet the Classic Period with unrestrained enthusiasm. After all, Mozart and Haydn were honest men. Furthermore, this was the period when great composers appeared and invented those forms that we cherish to this day.

Franz Joseph Haydn was born in 1732. Unfortunately, he invented nothing. When young Franz was but two years of age, his father took a good look at him.

For this reason, young Franz stayed home and met Bridgette Hissenbaum in 1753.[1]

Born in 1741, Bridgette was only two years old when her father, Heinrich, and her mother, Klementine,[2] realized that their daughter was a child prodigy. They found little Bridgette composing simple songs to the accompaniment of the ophicleide, one of which began as follows.

> *And she breathed in husky whisper:—*
> *"Curfew must not ring to-night."*

Bridgette was immediately given lessons in harmony, counterpoint, and on the ophicleide, and by the time she was four years of age, she was taken on a tour of Eastern Europe. Upon her return to Germany, she was appointed principal ophicleidist in the Mannheim Symphony Orchestra, and was acclaimed as one of the youngest female ophicleidists in Western Germany.

At Mannheim she also continued to compose simple songs which added to her fame. And in 1751 her first opera *Celemene* was produced, but unfortunately for Bridgette, it was not a success. As a matter of fact, Bridgette had begun to stutter in 1749, and as the following excerpt from her opera reveals, she found it exceedingly difficult to write simple dialogues.

HE: *Celemene, pray tell me,*
Pray, pray tell me, Celemene,
When those pretty, pretty, pretty Eyes I see,
Why my Heart beats, beats, beats, beats in my Breast,
Why, why it will not, it will not, why, why, it will
not let me rest:

SHE: *How should I know more than you?*
Yet would be a Woman too.
Nay, just now, nay, just now am pleased, am pleased
so well,
Should you, should you kiss me, I won't tell,

[1] At a church social in Cologne.
[2] Her maiden name was Schnitzer.

Should you, should you kiss me, I won't tell:
No, no I Won't tell, no, no I won't tell, no, no I won't tell.

HE: *My heart does so pant, pant, pant.*

It is fairly obvious to music scholars that stuttering operas have little chance for success, and Bridgette soon came to the same conclusion. For this reason she turned toward composing for instrumental ensembles that do not stutter, and in May of 1752 she composed her first string quartet. In June of 1752 she composed her first symphony. And in February of 1753, Bridgette Hissenbaum met Haydn as we have noted. Haydn was immediately fascinated by this beautiful stuttering girl and particularly by her string quartet and symphony that he took home and copied. She, in turn, was fascinated by Haydn as Dr. Steinglissinger's famous portrait of her indicates.

It is tragic that history must record the fact that Franz Joseph Haydn stole Bridgette Hissenbaum's string quartet and symphony and published them as his own. By doing this, he became known as the "Father of the String Quartet," and the "Father of the Symphony." And as Dr. Uz has pointed out, it is too bad that Bridgette Hissenbaum had no inclination to invent the football band march, for Haydn would then be known as the father of this too.[3] But more tragic is the fact that Bridgette Hissenbaum died from an overdose of aspirin when she learned that Haydn was a thief. Watteau's portrait of her remains as one of history's saddest commentaries.

[3] Johann Peter Uz, *Studien über Fussball Bands*, vol. 564, p. 23,906.

For this reason we turn sadly to Wolfgang Amadeus Mozart who copied the string quartet and symphony that Haydn had copied from Bridgette Hissenbaum. This, of course, leads us to the next century and to Beethoven who was an honest man.[4]

> *To summarize the development of music during the 1700's is to write the biography of Bridgette Hissenbaum. As her most famous biographer, Professor Hung Wun On wrote: "Who ran to help me when I fell, and would some pretty story tell, or kiss the place to make it well? My mother."*

---

[4] Spitzendorfer prefers to follow Mozart with Verdi, but as Dr. Uz wrote in his famous *Studien über Mozarts Vater und Mutter*, "*Horatio Spitzendorfer ist ein romantischer Esel!*" This may be translated roughly as, "A knave, a rascal; an eater of broken meats; a base, proud, shallow, beggardly, three-suited, hundred-pound, filthy, worsted-stocking knave."

14

ROMANTIC
MUSIC

I t is not easy for the mature music historian to approach the nineteenth century with complete objectivity. After having traced the history of music from *Pithecanthropus erectus* to Bridgette Hissenbaum, after having investigated the *bel canto* chests of Cretan women, after having examined medieval naked feet with dew on them, it is difficult for the thinking man to believe that much will happen in the Romantic period.

But as we have seen, page after page, the mature music historian is characterized by an indomitable will that forces him on and on—and for this reason there is no way to avoid Ludwig van Beethoven and those who followed him. It is as Dr. Steinglissinger's step-brother Dr. Reingold Stoneslider wrote; "O, yet we trust that somehow good will be the final goal of ill, to pangs of nature, sins of will, defects of doubt, and taints of blood." [1]

Beethoven was born in 1770 in the little hamlet of Biegelstadt.[2] As was the case with other composers of his century, he was an obnoxious person and, as might be expected, he was a

[1] Reingold Stoneslider, *History of Taints.*
[2] Now a suburb of Grossenbiegelstadt.

teen-age terror, clothed in his black leather jacket and poised on the back runner of his wildly flashing sled, both of which are depicted below.

Beethoven's father [3] recognized the fact that his son possessed no musical talents, but he also recognized the fact that his son might earn a little money for the family on concert tours. For this reason he gave young Ludwig lessons on the mandoline—but he never did take him on a tour of Western Europe.[4] Instead, the boy stayed home and studied thirteenth-century counterpoint with Wilhelm Rudolph Düsselschniffel. This was in 1783.

One of the great composers of all time, Düsselschniffel was born in 1769 and was immediately recognized as a musical genius by his father, Hermann, who taught his young son how to twirl a baton. At the age of three and one half, the talented youth was taken on a tour of Western Europe and the United States of America, and was acclaimed as the youngest baton twirler of that day. Upon his return to Germany he was appointed Professor of Baton Twirling and Football Band Music at the University of Biegelstadt.

Except for a few isolated works by such second-rate composers as Bach, Handel, Haydn, and Mozart, there is very little music composed specifically for baton twirling, and these lack a certain vital spark. For this reason, Düsselschniffel began to compose music which would be more suitable to the technique of a baton twirling virtuoso, and on July 4, 1776, he invented

[3] Who was also obnoxious.
[4] His father was never sober enough to travel.

the march for football band, his famous *Geschwindmarsch für Taktstocktriller und Fussball Orchester*, Op. 1, No. 1. This work was, of course, a landmark in music history, since it led directly to John Philip Sousa.[5]

Düsselschniffel performed his new composition at half time during the football game between the University of Regenguss and the University of Biegelstadt,[6] and it was so successful that he quit his job and concentrated on writing football band marches with baton twirling accompaniments. Nine hundred and fifty-seven of these marches are now available in a Roumanian edition.[7] Of additional interest to twentieth-century football band directors is the fact that all of Düsselschniffel's marches for baton twirlers and football bands are written in the key of C major, and are therefore excellent for football bands containing all C instruments.[8]

In 1777, Düsselschniffel was invited to the United States by Harvard University to lecture on baton twirling and to establish a high standard football band curriculum in conjunction with its Bachelor of Music program. He remained at Harvard for two years, teaching baton twirling and giving master classes in the organization of football bands to musicians from all over the United States and Canada, but he grew homesick for Biegelstadt and sailed for home in May of 1779. He left the United States, however, secure in the knowledge that all American colleges and universities[9] would soon have high standard baton twirling courses coordinated with their football band curricula.

Five years after his return to Biegelstadt, he met Beethoven, as we have seen. This obnoxious young man in the black leather

[5] Who may not be discussed later in this book.
[6] On October 18, 1776. Biegelstadt won by a score of 87 to 3, but they gave unlimited football scholarships.
[7] Copies may be obtained by writing to the Soviet Embassy in Washington, D.C. and enclosing 7,579,364 Kopecks. No trading stamps will be accepted.
[8] Bands consisting of tonettes and autoharps may enjoy them too, but allow plenty of rehearsal time.
[9] And high schools and grade schools.

jacket studied with Düsselschniffel for seventeen years and finally composed his first work in 1800. This composition, *Gassenhauer in F Moll für Taktstocktriller und Fussball Orchestra*, Op, 1, No. 1, cannot be classified as a mature work, and is seldom performed today, but it does illustrate the fact that Beethoven was still under Düsselschniffel's influence.[10]

Beethoven worked hard the following fifteen years with Düsselschniffel, but no other compositions came from his pen. He did not seem to possess the divine spark.[11] Finally in 1815 he moved to Vienna where he chanced to meet Katharina Pfeffernusse, the famous conductor of the female string orchestra at the Hofbrau, a small restaurant on the outskirts of the city. It was fortunate for musical posterity that she asked Beethoven to compose a theme song with which she might introduce her nightly dinner program, and the result is, of course, known to all of us: the beautiful *Mondschein Sonate für Fräuleinischeorchester* which was later arranged for piano.[12]

Unfortunately, Beethoven had drained his inspiration dry[13] and composed no more. Gasselwein published a collection of works in 1873 that were reputed to have been composed by Beethoven, but Dr. Henrik Snoilsky proved conclusively that Gasselwein was in error. It is only necessary to point out a few of the facts concerning Gasselwein's dishonesty: (1) Beethoven's so-called "nine symphonies" were written by Sophie Regenbogen, a pupil of Bridgette Hissenbaum; (2) Beethoven's so-called "sixteen string quartets" were written by Oswald Britschenhauer, a pupil of Sophie Regenbogen; (3) the so-called "five piano concertos" were composed by Bessie Brown, a pupil of Oswald Britschenhauer; (4) and Beethoven's so-called *Missa solemnis* was composed by Ito Watanabe, a pupil of Bessie Brown.

[10] The myth of Haydn's and Mozart's influence on Beethoven should be abandoned once and for all.

[11] He was also lazy.

[12] With two ugly movements added to it.

[13] Serious scholars frequently use the more appropriate expression: "Shot his wad."

To attribute these masterpieces to the composer of the *Gassen-hauer in F Moll für Taktstocktriller und Fussball Orchester* and the *Mondschein Sonate für Fräuleinischeorchester* is manifestly ridiculous.[14] The only thing that may be called genuine in Beethoven's case is his likeness in William Blake's famous portrait

---

[14] Gasselwein has just issued a new edition of these works "by Ludwig van Beethoven," but music historians know him to be unbelievably bullheaded. One may only recall his speech to the American Bridgette Hissenbaum Society when he shouted, "I propose to fight it out on this line if it takes all summer." We may also remember his opening sentence to this society: "The lips that touch liquor must never touch mine." Such stubborness does not wither easily.

above, which reveals that Beethoven retained his teen-age maliciousness even in his old age.

This leads us, of course, to Franz Schubert who is known chiefly for his invention of *Schubert's Serenade* which is frequently performed at weddings, funerals, and at women's musical gatherings. Schubert also invented the *Lied*, the plural of which is *Lieder*.[15] Among these are the *Erlkönig*,[16] *Die Wetterfahne*,[17] *An die Freude*,[18] *Der Rattenfänger*,[19] and "Who is Sylvia?"[20]

When Franz Schubert was born in 1797, he displayed all of the signs of genius and was soon composing simple little songs, one of which begins as follows.

> *Who killed Cock Robin?*
> *"I," said the Sparrow,*
> *"With my bow and arrow,*
> *I killed Cock Robin."*

His parents could also see, however, that he was not a boy to be trusted and, in fact, had a mean streak in him. For this reason, they enrolled him immediately in the "Konvict," a reformatory on the outskirts of Berlin. Unfortunately, Schubert did not improve during his stay in the reformatory and, indeed, his contact with other mean children who had no compunction about killing robins caused him to become even more morose and sullen. The last straw was Beethoven's visit to the reformatory. Schubert bought himself a black leather jacket also, and became known as the boy who carried a razor and a switch-blade knife in his hip pocket. The photograph of him in his jacket, duck-

---

[15] The North German word for "leader," a horse placed in advance of others.

[16] Young music historians are warned that the translation of this word as "Oil King" by Joe McGinnis, the Brooklyn music historian, is not correct.

[17] "The Wetting Faun."

[18] Dedicated to Sigmund Freud.

[19] "The Rotten Finger."

[20] We don't know. Neither did Schubert.

tailed haircut and dangling cigarette, still hangs in the reformatory's social hall and is reproduced below.

Although Schubert continued to compose simple little songs, the words that he used illustrate only too clearly the bitter hardness that was clasping his heart. We see this in the following beginning of one of his songs.

> *'Cause I's wicked,—I is.*
> *I's mighty wicked,*
> *Anyhow, I can't help it.*

And the early streak of cruelty toward birds only grew larger as the years passed.

> *Sing a song of sixpence, a pocket full of rye,*
> *Four-and-twenty blackbirds baked in a pie.*

To emphasize this cruel streak of his, Schubert never signed his name as normal people would. Instead, he drew a picture of an open razor and a poor little dead bird.

For all of these reasons, we must move on to Hector Berlioz who did not have a cruel hair on his head, as the famous portrait of him indicates.

Born in 1803,[21] Berlioz has been one of the most maligned composers of all time. This started, of course, with Hosenheimer's malicious biography of Berlioz in which he accused the shy young Frenchman of wearing elevator shoes and a corset.[22] Although Luigi Spumoni's research demolished Hosenheimer's contentions, the damage was done, and to this day school children all over the world still believe that Hector Berlioz wore

[21] Six years before Charles Darwin.
[22] Alexius Hosenheimer, *Berlioz und die Höheschuhe.*

elevator shoes and a corset. And the libel continues to grow.

As Dr. Spumoni proved,[23] Berlioz never wore elevator shoes until 1806 when he fell in love with Christine Coup de Dents who was six inches taller than he, and as Dr. Spumoni also demonstrated, it was *she* who wore the corset as the following portrait of her reveals.

[23] Luigi Spumoni, *Studien über Berliozs Schuhe*, vol. 783, p. 8,902.

Unfortunately, Christine Coup de Dents married another man in 1809, and Berlioz never wore shoes again and, in fact, inspired Edgar Allen Poe to write that poem loved by all:

> *Blessings on thee, little man,*
> *Barefoot boy, with cheek of tan!*
> *With thy turned-up pantaloons,*
> *And thy merry whistled tunes.*

Hector Berlioz then turned to music and in 1830 launched himself on a career as a composer of quiet and restful music with his *Symphonie fantastique*. But this restrained composition, scored for a small chamber orchestra of thirteen players, was not well received by the Parisian critics who accused Berlioz of imitating Haydn.

It is very probable that this harsh criticism would have crushed the mild-mannered young man if he had not met Abigail Morley, a dancer in Shakespeare's *Hamlet* being performed in Paris at that time.[24] This was, in fact, the turning point in Berlioz's life.[25]

We know from his letters[26] that Hector loved Abigail with an introverted anguish and that he longed to pour out his soul to her in song.[27] Nevertheless, he was too shy to dedicate his music to her openly.

Fortunately, Abigail's brother (Harold) was also in Paris at

[24] The French have always insisted that ballet be included in all plays and operas.
[25] Amedio Avocado, *Studien über Abigail Morley*, vol. 247, p. 4,938.
[26] See Hector Berlioz, *Mes lettres*, 94 vols. One should note in particular his one hundred and tenth letter to Abigail that begins: "*Comment allez-vous? Quelle heure est-il? Voulez-vous bien m'indiquer ou se trouve les lavabos?*" This, of course, is difficult to express in English but a rough translation may be, "The wanton boy that kills a fly shall feel the spider's enmity."
[27] He was always too broke to do it any other way.

this time,[28] and Berlioz began to dedicate his compositions through Harold. Among these are the well-known *Harold in Italy* for harp and viola,[29] the opera *Harold and Juliet*,[30] and in particular the famous *King Harold Overture*.[31] Tragically, however, Abigail married another man in 1860,[32] and Berlioz laid down his pen and composed no more. As Dr. Stumpfnose's astonishing research disclosed, Berlioz emigrated to the United States and was hung as a cattle rustler in Billings, Montana. Matthew Brady's photograph of this sad end is as follows.

[28] Harold Morley traveled extensively in Europe and North America for a sauce company. See Karl Stumpfnose's *Geschichte der Worcestershire Sauce* of which fifty-four volumes have already appeared. The remaining twenty-three volumes are due to be published this coming summer. As Dr. Stumpfnose wrote in the Preface of volume one of the English translation, "What this country really needs is a good five-cent cigar."

[29] This trip of Harold's to Italy is also described by the minor English poet, Lord Byron.

[30] Based on Beckenschmidt's 1631 edition of William Shakespeare's plays.

[31] This work not only honored Abigail's brother, but also King Harold of England who was killed by an arrow through his right eye at the historic Battle of Hastings in 1066. For further details concerning King Harold's left eye, see Dr. Stumpfnose's *Studien über Harolds Augen* which has also been published in a two-volume English translation: Vol. I. *Studies Concerning Harold's Right Eye;* Vol. II. *Studies Concerning Harold's Left Eye.* In this connection, Dr. Stumpfnose pointed out that Berlioz's music was in error when it described the type of arrow used by the Normans to kill King Harold.

[32] George Worcestershire, the president of her brother's sauce company.

This, of course, leads us to Fréderic Chopin.[33] Born in 1810,[34] Chopin wrote entirely for the piano because he was not musical enough to perform on the sackbut, Krummhorn, or dudelsack. As a matter of fact, he never really learned to play the piano well.[35] About all we can do is to look at his portrait which was painted by Degas in 1840 when Chopin was afraid that he was going to be shipped back to Poland by the French authorities.

Although Chopin's parents realized that their son was no child prodigy, they did recognize his limited talents for musical composition. The latter might have developed if he had not met Mme Amandine Lucile Aurore Dupin Dudevant who masqueraded shamelessly in trousers as the minor novelist, George Sand. Unfortunately, Chopin accompanied her to the island of Majorca— and that was the end of Fréderic Chopin.[36] Only two of his

[33] We'll get to Verdi sooner or later.
[34] Seventy-eight years after George Washington.
[35] His legs were too short to reach the pedals.
[36] Dr. Reinhold Glotsch wrote as follows in his *Studien über Georg Sand:* "*Armer Fréderic. Er war kaput!*" This may be translated as, "Poor Frederick. He was kapoot!"

compositions are performed in the twentieth century.[37] This leads us, of course, to Robert Schumann.[38]

Schumann was born in 1810 [39] and almost immediately began to write love letters to Clara Wieck, the daughter of his harmony and counterpoint teacher. And almost immediately, she wrote back.[40] For this reason his mother decided to send him to law school.[41] Unfortunately, the Law School at the University of Stuttgart could not afford to hire eminent piano teachers and Schumann was forced to study with the Italian-German teacher, Emilio Bosch, who broke Schumann's fingers with a finger-strengthening device. Schumann's left hand and the device is below.

[37] The *Revolutionary Etude* and the *Minute Waltz*. Both have been played inclusively by the well-known Danish music historian, Dr. Victor Borge, who wrote as follows in his famous book, *Chopin og Jeg: "Chopin opførte sig ikke godt."* This may be translated as, "Yon Cassius has a lean and hungry look."

[38] Maybe we'll get to Verdi.

[39] Ten years before General William Tecumseh Sherman.

[40] See her famous work, *Meine Briefe*, in one hundred and four volumes. Note, in particular, the ninety-seventh letter which begins as follows: *"Lieber Fréderic: Ich glaube dass Du ein Esel bist."* This may be translated roughly as: "Take thy beak from out my heart and take thy form from off my door! Quoth the Raven, 'Nevermore!'"

[41] So that he could defend himself in breach of promise suits.

For this reason, Schumann left us but one inspired composition, the famous *Träumerei* for cello and piano.[42] This leads us, of course, to Felix Mendelssohn.[43]

Mendelssohn was born in 1809,[44] and composed only two

[42] Which is performed frequently at garden parties and student recitals.
[43] We may be getting closer to Verdi.
[44] Five years after Aaron Burr shot Alexander Hamilton.

works: the *Spring Song* for maypole dancers in Berlin, and the *Songs Without Words* for singers who never went beyond the third grade. Mendelssohn is best known through his portrait painted by Gainsborough, a minor English artist of the time.

Unfortunately, this leads us to very little. Rossini was interested only in haircuts and shaves, Bizet in cigarette factories, and Saint-Saëns in swans. There is not very much material here for the mature music historian who would prefer to discuss more profound matters.

Fortunately, Franz Liszt was born in 1811.[45] From the time of his birth, he wore his hair shoulder length and his black eyes flashed forth from under his brows. His parents noticed this and immediately sent young Franz out to herd the family sheep. It was at this time that he met Phillis who delivered water to the village inn and the young man burst at once into song, the words of which begin as follows.

> *Phillis on the new made hay*
> *On a pleasant Summer's day*
> *She in a wanton posture lay*
> *   Thinking no Shepherd nigh her*
> *Till Amintas came that way*
> *   And threw himself down by her.*

Phillis was immediately attracted by the young man's face and her song is still performed regularly on the recital hall stage. It begins as follows:

> *I grow mad at his thin, gasping breath,*
> *While the black blood drips down on the pale ivory,*
> *And his eyeballs lie quenched with the weight of his brows*

Manet's famous photograph of Phillis carrying water is reproduced on the facing page for mature readers.

When Franz's parents heard his song and saw Phillis's picture they sent young Franz immediately to Vienna where there were

[45] Five hundred and eleven years after Guillaume de Machaut.

no sheep. He was given lessons in harmony and counterpoint by Professor Ernst von Bittersdorf, the court organist, and it was here that Liszt began to compose songs about ladies of higher station. He also gave them music lessons. He enjoyed the latter so much that he quit composing and just gave lessons. For this reason, we turn now to Richard Wagner who was interested solely in himself—and in his friends' wives.

Wagner was born in 1813, as was the British-Italian composer Joe Green.[46] Of all nineteenth-century composers, Richard Wagner was undoubtedly the most modest, unassuming, and altruistic, and for this reason, scholars enjoy discussing him.[47]

But there is more than joy in discussing this modest but great man, because with Wagner the story of music comes to a halt. No further developments are possible, and as we shall see, the history of twentieth-century music is simply the history of complete and abject degeneration and decay. This is confirmed time and again by all of the leading mature twentieth-century music historians.

Six months after he was born, Wagner's father (a policeman) died, and his mother married one of their boarders, a man named Geyer.[48] Wagner's mother and the boarder did not realize that the child was a musical genius because he was more interested in reading Greek books that he borrowed from the Leipzig public library. And at the age of four he translated his first Greek poem into English, the beginning being as follows.

> *A soft kiss Demo gives, but Doris bites,*
> *Daphne's is loud and long. Which most excites?*

When Wagner's mother and the boarder saw this, they canceled his subscription to the public library and bought him a

---

[46] Who is discussed later.

[47] Friedrich Nietzsche, the philosopher, also enjoyed discussing Wagner. In a letter to the composer in 1877, Nietzsche summed up the good will felt by all men: "*Wagner, Du bist ein Dummkopf.*"

[48] Who had just moved in.

trombone. Fortunately his right arm was longer than that of most children his age and he progressed rapidly on the instrument despite having no teacher. By the time he was six years old, Wagner was appointed principal trombonist in the Leipzig opera orchestra and, thus, was one of the youngest operatic trombonists in Germany. And it was at this time that he met Wilhelmina Planer, a very high soprano.[49] It was at this time also that Wagner had his portrait painted by Gottlieb Holbein, and never paid for it. This painting clearly reveals Wagner's innate timidity.

In the meanwhile, Wagner became extremely morose because very few nineteenth-century operatic composers liked the trombone, and he had very little chance to keep up his lip. For this reason, he began to compose his own operas which used a great number of trombones. And then he married Wilhelmina, although he called her Minna.[50] He also bought a dog which he called Otto.[51] Fortunately, Millet painted a portrait of Otto in 1863.

[49] We do not know how high, but she must have been very high when she married Wagner.
[50] After the heroine of his opera, *Hiawatha und Minnehaha.*
[51] Otto was the last of a breed that originated in the Pleistocene.

It is too bad, but Wagner was not an instantaneous success as a composer because most people did not care for a great number of trombones in opera music. For this reason, he and Wilhelmina (and their dog, Otto) went to Paris where trombones were more popular. Unfortunately, trombones had gone out of style in Paris the preceding year and Wagner and Wilhelmina (and Otto) did not eat regularly. In May of that year Wagner was handcuffed and led to jail for debts.[52] Now Wilhelmina took in boarders, but Wagner's lawyer got him released on a habeas corpus before it was too late.[53]

And then, good fortune entered his life. His opera, *Rienzi*, was accepted for performance in Dresden. Its story is as follows.

> Cola Rienzi (a great-grandfather of Coca Rienzi, who founded a soft-drink company) had a sister (Irene) who was abducted by Orsinis, who had no sister and was, therefore, lonely. Adriano Steffano Colonna, the son of Steffano Colonna, tore Irene away from Orsinis, and by this time Irene was in bad shape. For no apparent reason, the fickle people in Rome shouted "Down with Rienzi" who had done nothing to them, and on top of this he was excommunicated which was almost too much for Irene. However, she encouraged him to give a

[52] He took Otto with him.
[53] Wagner had already had experience with boarders.

speech to the people who burned down the building that contained the balcony from which he spoke, and the opera ends as Rienzi, Irene, and all of their friends sing in the flames until there is no more oxygen.

Rienzi was so successful that Wagner could now afford to live in better surroundings. He bought a house, lined its walls with pink satin drapes, sprayed it with attar of roses which he also used as a hair tonic, and divorced Wilhelmina. He also bought a better dog whose portrait by Delacroix is reproduced here.

Wagner then took in as a boarder Cosima, the wife of his good friend, Hans von Bülow. Next he wrote *The Flying Dutchman* which was produced at Dresden in 1843. We do not know who sang the leading role, but the story is as follows:

A very stubborn Dutchman swore that he would sail forever unless he found a woman who would be faithful to him. This woman was Senta who worked at a loom in a cotton mill, but she did not know about him yet. She worked at her loom for many years and one day the foreman of the mill showed Senta a picture of the Dutchman, and she liked it very much. She left Erick, her husband, joined the Dutchman the next time he sailed by, and then she threw herself into the sea because he was obnoxious and was so stubborn that he would not tell her his name. We still do not know it.

For obvious reasons, *The Flying Dutchman* was not a success, and so Wagner lost his new dog.[54] He did not lose Cosima, however, and she encouraged him to write a new opera which he called *Tannhäuser*. This was a different type of opera because

[54] He could not keep up with the payments.

the hero, Tannhäuser, was a Minnesinger from Minnesota.[55] It was performed in 1845, but as we can see below, the plot was so confusing that even Wagner did not understand what was going on.

Venus, who was called Holda in Germany, lived in a cave in Venusberg, which was called Hörselberg in Germany, and she lured Tannhäuser (who was also called Tannhäuser in Germany) to her cave. When the opera opens we see Venus (Holda) reclining with Tannhäuser while nymphs sway back and forth to the strains of voluptuous music, and a chorus of bacchantes dance in the background. In the far background we also see naiads bathing in a lake (but they are too far back for us to really see them), and even further back are some sirens floating on the surface of what looks like water. Tannhäuser had never encountered anything quite like this in Minnesota, and it was almost too much for him. However, he adjusts the best he can and the next morning he leaves Venusberg (Hörselberg) and goes to Rome which was about the only place that could save him now. After visiting Rome, he feels better and returns to the Castle of Wartberg where his fiancée, Elizabeth has been waiting for eighteen years.

Tannhäuser is rather surprised to see that Elizabeth is a little older, but he embraces her anyway. At about this point, the story becomes so confusing that no one knows what is happening. We can only say that Tannhäuser would have been better off if he had gone back to Venusberg (Hörselberg)—but he didn't.

After *Tannhäuser*, Wagner lost his house.[56] But he kept Cosima who encouraged him to write *Lohengrin* which was the first opera in which a swan is utilized as a means of transportation. For this reason, it was very successful as the following story may suggest.

Count Friedrich von Telramund accuses Elsa of murdering her brother (Gottfried), but the swan brings a mysterious knight (Lohengrin, of course) to her rescue, and they are married

[55] This is explained in considerable detail earlier on some previous page. It has been some time since this writer wrote it.

[56] The bank foreclosed on the mortgage.

(Elsa and Lohengrin. The swan was already married.). Lohengrin, however, had not traveled much in the world as we can see by the fact that he did not arrive on a horse, and he did not know much about women. He tells Elsa that she must never ask him for his name, but after they are married, she asks him for his name—and so he leaves on the swan. Elsa dies (she had it coming to her) and the swan turns into her lost brother who had become tired of carrying Lohengrin around on his back.

After the success of *Lohengrin*, Wagner was able to buy another house, and he immediately set to work on his next opera, *Tristan und Isolde*. Except for the fact that there is no swan in this opera, the story is about the same. For this reason there is no need to outline it here.

And as the German public had grown fond of swans, they did not care for *Tristan und Isolde*, so Wagner lost his house and dog again. Fortunately, Cosima did not leave him and she encouraged him to write *The Mastersingers of Nuremberg* which was produced in 1868 at Munich where Wagner, Cosima, and a new dog had moved in with her father, Franz Liszt. But this opera was not successful either. No one died and there was still no swan. However, before Cosima could take in boarders, Wagner wrote the *Ring of the Nibelung* which consisted of four operas in which everyone died.

The first of these, *The Rhine Gold*, has no plot, but the second opera, *The Valkyrie*, has enough plot to make up for it.

Wotan, king of the gods, visits the earth and meets Erda, an earth goddess, who gives birth to twins (Siegmund and Sieglinde). But they do not know that they are twins because Sieglinde immediately marries Hunding, and Siegmund goes off to fight Hunding's friends. Siegmund is wounded and drags himself to a hut which just happens to belong to Hunding and Sieglinde. However, Hunding is not home, but Sieglinde is. Siegmund and Sieglinde still do not know that they are twins and fall in love. Hunding comes home, but according to the current rules of hospitality, he must allow Siegmund to remain in his home overnight. This is too bad because Sieglinde drugs

Hunding, and Siegmund draws Wotan's sword from an oak tree which proves that Siegmund and Sieglinde are twins. But it is too late. Siegmund and Sieglinde flee from the house the next morning with Hunding in hot pursuit. Wotan wants to let Siegmund kill Hunding, but Flicka (the keeper of marriage vows and chastity) won't allow this. Brünnhilde is to see that Siegmund is slain, but she doesn't want to. Wotan then lets Hunding kill Siegmund and then kills Hunding, himself. Brünnhilde (no one knows who she is or where she came from so suddenly) is punished by being placed in a deep sleep and ringed with fire. Sieglinde, however, is spared so that Siegfried, her child by Siegmund, may be born. Otherwise, there would be no third opera.

The third opera, *Siegfried*, concerns the man of the same name who has now grown up and who falls in love with Brünnhilde who is considerably older than he is. Despite this, Siegfried rescues her from the ring of fire and carries her away in his carriage, a reproduction of which is as follows.

Siegfried was a very popular opera and Wagner earned a great deal of money from it. As a result, he, Cosima, and the dog moved out of her father's apartment, and bought a home which was draped in pink silk satin and sprayed with attar of roses.

The fourth, and last, opera of the *Ring* is called *Götterdämmerung* in German, and *The Twilight of the Gods* in English.[57] This was the most successful of all because Siegfried grew tired

[57] For no reason, whatsoever.

of being married to an older woman and was killed by Brünnhilde's oldest brother, Hagen, who caught him with Gutrune, his youngest daughter. After that there was little for Brünnhilde to do but throw herself on the fire in which Hagen was slowly roasting Siegfried. Nothing was left of Siegfried except for his coat and left shoe, both preserved for posterity by Professor Percy Pugh and reproduced below.

Wagner had made enough money by this time to quit while he was ahead, but his innate greed led him to write *Parsival* which is really an oratorio, and therefore will not be discussed in this book. For this reason, we finally move on to the British-Italian composer Joe Green.

Joe was born, as we have already noted, in 1813, the year of Wagner's birth. At this time, Joe's parents lived in the English section of Spizza, a small town near Busseto, Italy. However, in 1814 the family moved to the Italian section and the father was required to change his name from John Green to Giovanni Verdi, and Joe's to Giuseppe.[58]

Giovanni realized immediately that Giuseppe was a child prodigy and sent him to study the fluegelhorn with the conductor of the municipal band in Busseto. At the same time, the

[58] English music historians have tried desperately to keep him Joe, but with no luck.

young man was composing simple little Italian songs which were sung by Italians, young and old. However, in June of the following year,[59] a traveling opera company visited Busseto and performed Wagner's *Flying Dutchman*, and this had a tremendous impact upon the young boy. He no longer had a desire to compose simple little Italian songs or marches for the Busetto municipal band. He wanted to write operas. Particularly, Wagnerian operas.

Unfortunately, Italian audiences did not care for Wagnerian operas, and despite the Wagnerian beauty in the overtures of such works as *Rigoletto, Il Trovatore,* and *La Traviata,* Verdi

achieved no success and could not even buy a dog. Only the Quartet from *Rigoletto* has retained some notoriety due to Cézanne's well-known painting. (For financial reasons, Verdi was forced to sing in his own operas, and he may be seen third from the left in the picture.) Finally, he received a commission from the Khedive of Egypt,[60] to write an Egyptian opera, and

[59] We are not sure which year this is.
[60] Abdul the Bulbul Amir.

although it did contain one or two pleasant Italian folk-like melodies, no one came to see it. Not even the Khedive. As this maligned, yet thoroughly enjoyable, work is no longer performed, its story is as follows:

Amonasro, the King of Ethiopia, declared war on Tutmosis, the King of Egypt. Tutmosis won, and Amonasro's daughter, Aïda, is taken as a slave and given to Amneris, the daughter of Tutmosis. Rhadames, Tutmosis's best general, used to love Amneris, but now loves Aïda. Amonasro declared war again and Rhadames captures him without knowing that Aïda is Amonasro's daughter. Amneris is rather slow-witted, but she finally suspects that Rhadames does not love her any more, but loves Aïda instead. This makes Amneris angry. However, Tutmosis congratulates Rhadames for capturing Amonasro and offers Amneris to him (Rhadames, not Amonasro). But Rhadames does not want Amneris, and for this reason both Amneris and Tutmosis are angry—particularly, Amneris. And so Rhadames and Aïda (who may or may not have been consulted) were sealed in a cement vault with just enough oxygen to allow them to sing one final duet. Unfortunately, there was no swan in this opera, either.

Verdi quit writing operas and became an engineer on the through-train between Moscow and Tokyo. Benvenuto Cellini's famous painting of this train is reproduced here.

This leads us, of course, to Claude Debussy who rebelled against Wagner's romantic operas with their medieval stories, tales of immortality, and mass suicides. Born in 1862, Debussy was immediately recognized as a child prodigy by his parents, and, as we know from the well-known portrait painted by Claude Monet, Mrs. Debussy gave her young son piano lessons at an early age (his early age).

On his third birthday, young Debussy wrote his only important composition, *Clair de lune*, which enables the children of the world to give piano recitals for their parents and close friends.

During his remaining years, Debussy composed background music exclusively for film studios in Hollywood, and although most of these scores have been allowed to decay, a few are still heard whenever old movies are shown on television: *Il pleure dans mon coeur* ("It is raining in my heart"), *Suite Bergamasque* ("Sweet Burgomaster"), *Sirens* ("Fire Sirens"), *La mer* ("The

Old Gray Mare"), and *Soupir* ("Soup").[61] Two other film scores are heard occasionally: *Et la lune descend sur le temple qui fut* ("And the loon descends on the temple which foot"), and *La fille aux cheveux de lin* ("The girl on the linen horse").

Before he died, Debussy wrote one opera, *Pelleas et Melisande*, in order to correct all of Wagner's mistakes: medievalism, gloom, death—and as we have seen above, immorality. Its story is as follows:

> Melisande is lost in the gloomy woods near a medieval castle, but she is found by Golaud who immediately marries her—after finding a minister behind one of the trees. Golaud takes Melisande back to his castle where his half-brother, Pelleas, is waiting. Golaud, who had not traveled a great deal in the world, did not know why Pelleas was waiting, but he soon found out. When he did, he killed Pelleas and finally Melisande died in the last act. There is no swan in this opera either.

This leads us, of course, to Maurice Ravel, who was born in 1875. Ravel composed the *Bolero*, and this leads us to the twentieth century when things can only get worse.[62]

> *The world-famous authority on nineteenth-century music Dr. Olga Ussopov sees no reason for entering the present century and, in fact, she says, "Woodman, spare that tree! Touch not a single bough! In youth it sheltered me, and I'll protect it now."*

[61] Adopted as the theme song for the famous radio program sponsored by the well-known maker of 57 varieties.

[62] Bissenbaumenschweitzer misinterpreted Dr. Julius Thatcher when he quoted the latter as saying: "*Lass uns nach Hollywood gehen. Die Hollywoodische Busen sind wunderbar.*" Reference to Dr. Thatcher's treatise, *Studien über Hollywoodische Busen*, proves conclusively that his true statement was: "*Lass uns nach Hollywood gehen. Die Hollywoodische Busen sind falsch—aber wunderbar.*" This, of course, may be translated as: "Let us to Hollywood go. Hollywood bosoms are false—but wonderful."

15

TWENTIETH-
CENTURY MUSIC

he history of twentieth-century music has never been written, chiefly—as we have seen—because after Richard Wagner, it became impossible for composers to go any further. Everything musical had been invented, as this book has indicated clearly. However, a scholarly treatise must not be published incomplete, and for that reason, this chapter will deal with twentieth-century music in great detail.

Scholars know, however, that there is no twentieth-century music of any importance outside the national boundaries of the United States, Canada, and Quebec; for this reason, the present writer will give his American readers a complete and accurate account of the development of North American music from its beginnings at the hands of the Potawatomi.[1]

We are indebted to the famous American music historian Dr. Henry Wadsworth Longfellow for a detailed account of these beginnings, and there is no doubt that all Americans owe a

[1] Readers from other countries may as well turn back to Chapter One and start all over again, although the remaining pictures may interest them mildly.

great debt of gratitude to him for bringing to our attention the creative talents of Hiawatha Nawadaha, the first native-born American composer. But, of course, most of our gratitude must go to Dr. Steinglissinger's grandson, Dr. Lohengrin Stoneslider, for his translation of Dr. Longfellow's treatise which was, naturally, written in the Potawatomi dialect. We are also indebted to Dr. Stoneslider for his portrait of Hiawatha which reveals that creative character unique to Hiawatha.

Although Hiawatha was undoubtedly a fine composer, it is apparent that he was also cruel. As Dr. Longfellow tells us, Hiawatha walked "proudly" with his bow and arrows, and although the birds said to him, "Do not shoot us, Hiawatha," and the squirrel pleaded with him, "Do not shoot me, Hiawatha," and even the little rabbit whispered to him, "Do not shoot me, Hiawatha," Hiawatha shot them. And as Dr. Stoneslider's portrait of one of the little birds indicates (next page), no truly significant composer could ignore its pleadings.

This leads us, of course, to more humane American composers. Captain John Smith, the first mayor of Jamestown, Virginia, has often been cited as a performer on the cello, but his own account informs us clearly that the only musicians in Jamestown at that time were some Potawatomi who tried to use his head as a kettledrum tuned in B flat.[2]

We know that the Pilgrims landed at Plymouth in 1620, but despite the efforts of certain minor music historians, no evidence has been uncovered that Pilgrim fathers or mothers could whistle any tune except "Old Hundreth." And, according to the early American music scholar, Dr. Cotton Mather, they could not whistle this in the right key.[3]

Maryland was founded in 1634 by Cecilius Calvert, but instead of encouraging his people to learn music, he established a whiskey factory. It did, however, cause Maryland to become the home of distinguished gentlemen.[4]

It was not until we reach 1859 that we find one glimmer of honest musical activity in the United States or Canada of which one can be proud. This glimmer was reported in the *Bangor Gazette*, a monthly newspaper published in Bangor, Maine, by Hattie Thistlewaite.[5] A one-sentence crumb of hope, it reads as follows: "At the last concert of Fiske's Cornet Band,

---

[2] Kussbein stated that the note was B natural, but his argument was demolished by Dr. Grossbust.

[3] As Dr. Mather wrote in his famous treatise, "But yet the pity of it, Iago! O Iago, the pity of it, Iago!"

[4] See *Time* magazine, vol. 25, no. 7, p. 56, the Canadian edition.

[5] She became a Mexican citizen in 1818.

Miss Jenny Twichell, the daughter of our leading family, sang 'The Last Rose of Summer' to an overflow audience of seventeen people."

Now if this is true—and to doubt Hattie Thistlewaite's integrity is to demonstrate one's lack of scholarship—it certainly speaks well for Bangor's musical tastes, although it is possible, of course, that Fiske's Cornet Band performed light works on its part of the program.

We do know, however, that Jenny Twichell became extremely famous as an interpreter of "The Last Rose of Summer," and the summit of her career was her recital of operatic arias and "The Last Rose of Summer" in Carnegie Hall.[6] After that, she retired from the stage and became a waitress in the Bangor Cafe where she sang "The Last Rose of Summer" nightly to the patrons. It was on one of these historic occasions that Gilbert Stuart painted the portrait we now have.

We now encounter a great gap in the history of North American music which even such music historians as Kussbein and Regenguss have not been dishonest enough to bridge. Absolutely nothing happened—even in Bangor—from 1859 to 1900. It is true that the *Walla Walla Herald* published a short announcement on Thursday, March 7, 1887, stating that Miss Sadie

[6] She rented it for $60.

Bunchgrass would sing the popular and beloved aria "The Last Rose of Summer" on the following Saturday, but a cloudburst wiped out the town the next day.[7]

For this reason, if a music historian possesses any moral fibre at all, he must move on to January 1, 1900. It was on this day that Homer Twichell, Jenny's grandnephew, was born in Azusa, California, and astounded his mother and father with his innate musical talents. Nor was there any need to give him instruction since he composed his first simple little song with harp accompaniment at the age of three months. As its final words indicate, Homer showed great promise.

> *The Shepherd caught her in his arms,*
> *And laid her on the brink,*
> *And what he did without delay,*
> *You know, or else may think.*

Homer's mother and father were somewhat concerned that he might be showing great promise too soon and that he might burn himself out at an early age. And he almost did, as Pierre la Bouche's famous painting indicates. They therefore enrolled

[7] Miss Bunchgrass has never been seen since. Nor has Walla Walla.

⊰{ 114 }⊱

him immediately in the Azusa Academy for Wayward Boys where he was issued a uniform and a knife. The academy authorities did allow him to retain his harp, however, and to this day, one may see the framed photograph taken of him by Hiram Whistler.

As this photograph indicates, Homer Twichell was not a typical teen-age terror, but, in fact, he possessed some ostensible sensitivity.

As Dr. Whistler pointed out, however, Homer Twichell had a few peculiarities that set him somewhat aside from his fellow wayward colleagues.[8] But the fact that he differed from some

[8] Dr. Hiram Whistler, *The History of Waywardness*, vol. 749, p. 65,720.

boys by playing with an old skull that he had found on one of his strolls, and that he kept a vulture as a pet should not blind us to his musical genius. Furthermore, as we can see, neither the skull nor the vulture were out of the ordinary.

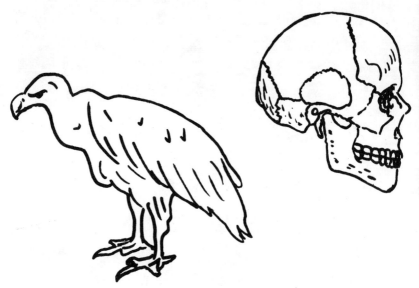

Actually, it was on an occasion when Homer Twichell was polishing the skull that the most significant event in music history occurred. As Dr. Hiram Whistler tells us in his work cited above, Homer Twichell sat in his cell one rainy Tuesday afternoon, shining his skull with an old tennis sock while he hummed the words of "The Hanging of Danny Deever." When he came to the line, "They tied thirteen knots into the rope for poor Danny Deever," Homer Twichell realized with a start that he had invented the Thirteen-Tone Method of musical composition, seven years before an obscure Austrian named Arnold Schoenberg invented the less important Twelve-Tone Method of musical composition.

Homer Twichell put down his skull and old tennis sock, climbed down three floors from his cell window, and ran into the business district of Azusa where he founded the famous

Azusa Conservatory of Thirteen-Tone Music.[9] The following day[10] he began to lecture to his many students [11] on his now-famous theory. First, he played the thirteen-tone scale for his students on his harp.

Then Homer Twichell explained how he had arranged these thirteen notes in something that he called a "tone row." In "The Hanging of Danny Deever" the tone row is as follows.

After he had played the tone row on his harp, he explained that each note of the tone row must be assigned a number—an Arabic number, *never* a Roman number.[12] But the most important feature of his method is that the notes of the tone row must always be used in consecutive order: forwards, backwards, upwards, downwards—and if the composer wishes to be even more profound—backwardsupsidedownwards and downwardsbacksideupwards.[13]

Thus, the final "hanging scene" from this historic composition begins as follows.

[9] In the old American Legion Hall on Main Street.
[10] Wednesday.
[11] Who had enrolled that morning.
[12] As Schoenberg, unfortunately, was to advocate many years later.
[13] These two terms are, of course, roughly translated from Homer Twichell's German, but the meaning should be clear.

Then it goes backwards.

Then, upwards and downwards.

And finally, backwardsupsidedownwards.

But not downwardsbacksideupwards, because Homer Twichell was saving that for his next thirteen-tone composition, the *Hanging of Miss Otis Regrets*, which he completed on Thursday, August 9, of that year.

These first two works were received with such immense enthusiasm by the Azusa audiences that Homer Twichell was literally besieged with offers from music publishing companies and community string quartets and symphony orchestras for his music as rapidly as he could compose it. For example, the following premieres were arranged during September of 1917 alone: *String Quartet No. 147* (Milton, Oregon); [14] *Thirteen*

[14] Performed by the Milton, Oregon Academy for Young Women String quartet: Kunigunde Zweischmidt, first violin, Philippine Schwachbein, second violin; Adelheiss Wurst, viola; and Friederike Schmiessenpfissel, cello. Julchen Kaffeelagen turned pages and ushered.

Steps to Parnassus, an opera in thirteen acts (Altus, Oklahoma);[15] *Symphony No. 189* (DeKalb, Illinois);[16] *Concerto for Thirteen Wind Instruments* (High Point, North Carolina);[17] and *The Hanging of Miss Otis's Brother* (Castlegar, British Columbia).[18]

The impact of Homer Twichell's thirteen-tone technique of composition was felt all over the world. Publishers scrapped their books that taught modal harmony, modal counterpoint, strict counterpoint, and traditional harmony and issued textbooks teaching the new thirteen-tone technique. And conservatories and music schools on all continents established new theory programs in which beginning students started with thirteen-tone sight-reading, thirteen-tone ear-training, thirteen-tone harmony, thirteen-tone counterpoint, thirteen-tone canon and fugue, and thirteen-tone form and analysis. Bach, Beethoven, Mozart, Brahms, Wagner—and even Bridgette Hissenbaum—were forgotten while Homer Twichell composed night and day to meet the terrific demand.

[15] Presented by the Elk City Oratorio Society, conducted by Dr. Reinhold Teufelskerl, seated at the Eilers upright piano. The leading roles were sung by Tullius Haarband, tenor (who was Lohengrin), and Luischen Bauch, soprano (who sang the part of Aïda). Sophie Lachkrampf turned pages, ushered, sold tickets, and poured tea at the reception.

[16] Performed in its entirety by the DeKalb Philharmonic Orchestra, conducted by Dr. Rudolph Tortenbäcker. Cäzilia Spiegeltisch turned pages. No one ushered or poured because no tickets were sold—and no one came.

[17] Performed by the King's Mountain Municipal Band, directed by Dr. Hans Gassbrenner at the ophicleide. Members of the ensemble were Adolph Gassbrenner, Andreas Gassbrenner, August Gassbrenner, Bartholomäus Gassbrenner, Christoph Gassbrenner, Ernst Gassbrenner, Franze Gassbrenner, Georg Gassbrenner, Gottfried Gassbrenner, Heinrich Gassbrenner, Humfried Gassbrenner, and Zacharias Gassbrenner. Lucia Gassbrenner was to sell tickets, usher, turn pages and pour spiked punch, but she couldn't. She had drunk the punch that morning.

[18] Performed by the Castlegar Unaccompanied Choral Society with the assistance of the Castlegar Brass Band, conducted by Dr. Bertram Fyfe-Drawbridge, A.R.C.B.I. (Dr. Fyfe-Drawbridge had received the diploma of Associate of the Royal College of Brass Instruments in 1857 with high honours.) Bertha Fyfe-Smith turned pages and ushered.

Fortunately, all of Homer Twichell's students at the Azusa Conservatory of Thirteen-Tone Music began to compose, and relieved some of the mounting strain from his courageous shoulders. And as they too became wealthy from the sale of their works, they started new conservatories in various parts of the world.[19]

With the mounting strain relieved from his courageous shoulders, Homer Twichell was finally able to marry his most talented student, Bessie Klanghart, who had been typing his lecture notes for three years and living in his basement rumpus room. On December 6, their daughter Myrtle was born. On December 9 Myrtle sat on her parent's kitchen floor and composed a simple little thirteen-tone song and Homer Twichell sang with joy in his heart [20]

Realizing that his daughter was, indeed, a musical genius, Homer Twitchell immediately began to give her lessons in the fourteen-tone technique which had, of course, superseded the old-fashioned thirteen-tone technique. When Myrtle was two years of age, her parents took her on a tour of Idaho, Wyoming, and Manitoba, where she astounded people with her ability to improvise on the organ fourteen-tone fugues based on cowboy songs whistled to her by members of the audience. By the time Myrtle was three, she had mastered the fifteen-tone technique which had, of course, superseded the fourteen-tone technique. By the time Myrtle was four, she had renounced the fifteen-tone technique and, on August 11, went to her room and locked the door.

For twenty-two years and seventeen days, Myrtle Twichell remained in her room and worked mysteriously. In the meanwhile, her mother ran away with the headmaster of the Azusa Academy for Wayward Boys, and her father invented the sixteen-tone technique of musical composition.

[19] The most famous being in Alep, Syria (the home of goat's wine), and Aalborg, Denmark (the home of acquavit).
[20] To the words of "Oh, frabjous day! Callooh! Callay!"

At the end of the twenty-second year and seventeenth day, Myrtle emerged from her room and knocked on her father's studio door. When he opened the door, Myrtle said, "Hello, Father," because she had not seen him for some time.

"Hello, Myrtle," he replied, because he had not seen her for some time either. And then he saw that she was carrying something in her hand.[21] "What do you have there?" he asked.

"A portable computer," she replied with a faint smile on her lips.[22] and she looked up into his face.[23]

With a faint smile on his face, he asked, "What is it for?" And he looked down into her face.[24]

Myrtle shifted her leg and with a faint smile on her face, she replied, "To compose with."

Her father shifted his leg and with the barest of smiles on his face asked, "Sixteen-tone music?"

Myrtle Twichell looked up into her father's face and said, "No, father. You are hopelessly out of date now." And she added with a faint smile on her face, "You're just not with it, Dad." And Myrtle Twichell set her portable computer on a table, took her place in front of it, pushed a button on the machine, and looked up into her father's bloodless face. As Gaughin's well-known portrait of Myrtle Twichell and her portable computer reveals, her father knew that she had spoken the truth. (See next page.)

Bitter cold stabbed Homer Twichell's heart, for he well knew that he was little more than a museum piece now that Myrtle's portable computer had made his sixteen-tone technique of musical composition obsolete. And with a faint smile on his face he turned and shuffled out of the room, went to the library, closed the door, opened the left drawer of his writing desk, and sat down.

[21] Her left one.
[22] Both of them.
[23] She was not quite sure that he was her father.
[24] He was not quite sure that she was his daughter.

Myrtle shifted her foot and waited. When she heard the shot, she shuffled back to her room carrying her portable computer and started to work on another composition. The following day, her neighbors heard an explosion and saw the Twichell house fall in ruins.[25]

This leads us, of course, to nothing else. After Myrtle Twichell's portable computer, nothing can come. Only a small bubble of hope lies waiting in the next chapter.

Only one musical scholar dares summarize the twentieth century with its minute bubble of hope waiting in the dim future. Elmer Springbuck's courage is, therefore, magnificent as he writes, "Why don't you speak for yourself, John?"

[25] Myrtle had pushed the wrong button.

16

A BUBBLE
OF HOPE

he ashes of Myrtle Twichell's home had not grown cold before a small bubble appeared in the Soviet Union. Writing in the May 17 Sunday supplement of the Communist Party newspaper, *Pravda*,[1] the prominent music historian, Sergei Karpovich Popoff, stated most categorically that Myrtle Twichell had been a "revisionist who had threatened Marxist dialectical materialism, but her destruction will now hasten the flowering of that truly twentieth-century musical art that sprang forth on the eve of the 1917 Revolution."[2]

Now Western historians may dispute part of Popoff's thesis, but his final statement staggers the scholarly mind: "Да! У меня в пра́вом у́хе звени́т."[3]

---

[1] The evening home edition.

[2] This was corroborated by the Rumanian music scholar Professor Ion Constantin Gigurto, who said, "We must all hang together, else we shall all hang separately."

[3] This may be translated literally as: "Where the bee sucks, there suck I; In a cowslip's bell I lie."

It must be obvious to the acutely tuned inquiring mind that there is a hidden meaning in Popoff's words, and, indeed, an analytical examination of his statement in its full Marxian context reveals the true meaning. In one fell swoop, Popoff relegates Jelly Roll Morton, Bob Dylan, The Beatles, and John Philip Sousa to historical oblivion by asserting that jazz, folk music, rock and roll—and even the football band march—were invented by Boris Rasputin, Dmitry Shiskov, The Bolsheviks, and Olga Pavlov respectively. Here, of course, is information that was bound to be contested hotly in some musical quarters, but Popoff's case appears to be airtight.

His arguments concerning the invention of jazz by Boris Rasputin are especially well documented and firm. Born of humble parents in southern Azerbaijan, Rasputin displayed an astounding childhood aptitude for music by providing the rhythm for balalaika bands at country hoe-downs in a neighbor's barn. Seated on a bale of hay, the youngster would perform the most intricate rhythmic patterns by striking his father's best sickle with a ball-peen hammer while the gay couples whirled by.[4]

In 1916 Rasputin's precociousness came to the attention of the Tsar who paid personally to send the boy to the Moscow Conservatory for instruction in advanced sickle and hammer playing. Unfortunately, young Rasputin's father could not spare his sickle and the boy studied anvil playing instead. After graduation, he became the principal anvilist in the court orchestra, and he was particularly acclaimed for his virtuosity in Verdi's *Anvil Chorus* (from the opera, *The Village Smithy*) and in Tchaikovsky's 1812 *Overture*.

Secretly, however, Rasputin longed for his old instruments, and immediately after receiving his first paycheck he sneaked

---

[4] To their favorite tune, "Turkey in the Straw," from Tchaikovsky's *Second Piano Concerto*.

out of the palace and bought a second-hand sickle and hammer at Bissenhoff's Pawn Shop.[5]

Each night after that he would hurry from the royal concert with his sickle and hammer to the Okhotsk Cafe where he and three friends (Leonidas, four-stringed zither; Mikhail, keyed bugle; and Markimovich, upright piano) would smoke marijuana (they called it "пот," that is, "pot") and improvise on the popular tunes from Glinka's operas. Night after night the small group ("комбо," as they said) smoked "пот," improvised ("фáкел") and practiced the new tunes that Rasputin composed. When the November Revolution arrived, Rasputin and his friends were ready.

On the night of November 27, 1917, celebrators rushed from the barricades and poured into the Okhotsk Cafe eager to dance to the Ragtime Jazz ("рагтйме джазз," they called it) of Comrade Rasputin and His Happy Four. Hour after hour the Happy Four played Rasputin's new compositions: "The Red Town Strutter's Ball," "The Lenin Rag," "The Balalaika Stomp," "The Trotsky Street Blues"—and most famous of all, "I Wish That I Could Shimmy Like My Sister Katrinka."

The success achieved by Rasputin and His Happy Four was phenomenal, and as Popoff proved conclusively in subsequent issues of *Pravda* (and substantiated by Rumanian, Lithuanian, and Latvian music historians), Western Imperialists began to form their own ragtime bands in rank imitation of Soviet esthetic ideology. Furthermore, the Americans even stole the Soviet jazz terminology in blatant defiance of international copyright laws.

---

[5] On Petrograd Street at that time, but subsequently renamed Lenin Avenue, then Stalin Boulevard, then Molotov Street, then Malenkov Avenue, then Bulganin Boulevard, then Khrushchev Street, then Brezhnev-Kosygin Avenue, then Brezhnev Boulevard, then—and then, we can't be sure.

A few examples will make the latter painfully clear. Comrade Igor Brobinsky invented the чарльстон in 1919; three years later the Yankee C Melody Saxophonist, Hiram Perkins, "invented" the "Charleston." Comrade Peter Trepoff invented свинг in the middle 1920's, but an anonymously decadent American "invented" an obvious imitation called "Swing" nearly ten years later. The Soviet Блакк Боттом of 1921 became the American "Black Bottom" of 1926. The Soviet keyed bugle player, Ivanovich Zuboff, invented Бебоп, to be followed obsequiously by an American with "Bebop." And the Soviet Биг Банд of the early 1920's was aped by the Americans in the 1930's when they "invented" the "Big Band." The list could be extended indefinitely.

Perhaps the crushing point of Popoff's thesis is the fact that Soviet jazz musicians (and college students) grew bored with pot in the early 1920's and turned to LSD, but it took the Western Imperialists over forty years to make the switch. All in all, even the most objective of Western music historians must accept this total picture with abject shame and remorse. They can only view Cézanne's well-known etching of Boris Rasputin's Communist victory gesture, and wince in a scholarly manner. (This etching was made in 1919, and the scholarly reader must be reminded that the clenched fist was not legalized until January of the following year.)

Fortunately, however, Popoff's contentions about folk music are not so unshakeable.[6] That Dmitry Shiskov did do pioneer work in this area must be admitted by all serious scholars, but to credit him with the *invention* of folk music does not set well in all academic circles.[7]

We know for certain that Shiskov was born no earlier than 1878 and thus it seems highly improbable that he was, indeed, the composer of such early folk songs as "Old MacDonald Had a Farm" or "Polly Wolly Doodle." [8] It is true that the Albanian music historian, Midhat Hoxha, maintained rather belligerently that Shiskov wrote these songs, as well as "Clementine," "On Top of Old Smoky," and the "Swiss Yodel Song," but Hoxha's flimsy arguments were demolished by Professor Koki Jujiwara in the latter's history of Kentucky.[9]

All in all, it seems probable that we can only accept Shiskov's authorship of the popular Russian folk song, "Short'nin' Bread," and it is barely possible that he did write the words to the famous Yugoslavian song "Three Blind Mice," but certainly not the melody.[10] For these reasons, the Western world can heave a momentary sigh of scholarly relief.

The Soviet invention of Rock and Roll, on the other hand, is an open and shut case. Popoff's documentation is ironclad. Three weeks after the initial success of Boris Rasputin and His Happy

[6] Piffendorf disagrees, but there has been some suspicion that he cast an absentee ballot for Adolf Hitler.

[7] Dr. Giusto Gozzi of the University of Pisa summed it up when he wrote, "Something is rotten in the state of Denmark."

[8] Doctoral candidates in music should examine Dr. Sven Jorgensen's article on doodling in the 1913 issue of the *Norwegian Farm Journal* where he wrote, "*Jeg elsker øl.*" As Norwegian-speaking scholars well know, this must be translated as, "Alas, they had been friends in youth, but whispering tongues can poison truth."

[9] See his *Histoire de la Kentuquy* in which he says, "*Je désire téléphoner,*" an assertion that may be translated as, " 'Twas the night before Christmas, when all through the house not a creature was stirring, not even a mouse."

[10] Which we now know was composed by Palestrina.

Four, five high school drop-outs climbed on their motorcycles (they called them "Horc," a word later to be "invented" by Americans as "hogs") and roared across Red Square in pursuit of baby buggies, old women, and cripples. While this innocent type of diversion seemed satisfying for a time, it soon palled, and the five drop-outs (Ilyich, Sontsovka, Ivan, Borisovich, and Igor) sold their Horc and bought a set of drums and four electric balalaikas. They also sent Ilyich, their leader, to the conservatory where he learned the three most important musical chords: C major, F major, and B double-sharp major.

Night after night for two days Ilyich, Sontsovka, Ivan, Borisovich, and Igor rehearsed—and on February 10 they were ready. Celebrators of all ages poured into the Trotsky Auditorium eager to hear Ilyich and The Bolsheviks, as they called themselves, play the new "рохк 'н ролл," or "Rock 'n Roll," as it was later plagiarized by the English. The music proved to be refreshingly loud and the immense audience cheered the Bolshevik's subtle use of the three chords and of their profound treatment of rhythm. Unfortunately the audience left after the first number and the crestfallen young artists found themselves facing one thirteen-year-old girl sitting alone in the auditorium. With her raven black hair framing her youthfully soft face, she sat, chewed her gum, and stared impassively at them. Slowly she rose to her feet and her words echoed throughout the hall: "Где ванная на этом этажé?" She then walked out of the auditorium.

Ilyich and his four companions packed up their instruments and strolled inconsolably to the Lenin Museum of Art. Mutely they walked through the rooms pausing to examine certain art masterpieces: Albrecht Dürer's *Portrait of the Artist as a Young Man*, Tagayoto's popular painting of *Sir Galahad*, Henry Wrigglesworth's priceless portrait of *General Custer*, and particularly Lucienne Montcalm's painting of *Kit Carson*. Finally the five young men sat down and held their heads in their hands. Ilyich was the first to speak. "She was right, Comrades. Our hair's too short."

Then Ivan raised his head and nodded. "Da." [11]

Sontsovka, Borisovich, and Igor rose slowly to their feet. "Da," [12] they said.

Six months later, Ilyich and The Bolsheviks were ready. Celebrators of all ages between twelve and fifteen poured into the Trotsky Auditorium eager to hear the true "рохк' н ролл" —and, as Sergei Karpovich Popoff said, the rest is history. Over thirty years later, Western Imperialists "invented" Rock 'n Roll, completely ignorant of the fact that The Bolsheviks had become bored with long hair and amplified balalaikas in 1925 and, in fact, had invented the barber shop quartet, or "Барбер шоп квартет," as they called it. (Ilyich never had been able to carry a tune, so they dropped him.)

Proof of this is amply demonstrated by Rodney Hepplewhite's famous photograph of The *New* Bolsheviks. It is shown below. [13]

[11] Loosely translated, this may be, "The plowman homeward plods his weary way, and leaves the world to darkness and to me."

[12] Loosely translated, this may be, " 'Tis not a lip, or eye, we beauty call, but the joint force and full result of all."

[13] This picture, which now hangs in the British Museum, was long mistaken for a portrait of Eton choir boys until Popoff revealed the truth.

As was the case with Dmitry Shiskov and folk music, there is grave doubt concerning Olga Pavlov's role in the invention of the football band march. It is true that she did do some pioneering in the field of baton twirling at the University of Stalingrad, but readers of this book know well that the true *inventor* of baton twirling *and* of the football band march was Beethoven's teacher, Wilhelm Rudolph Düsselschniffel.

Nevertheless, scholars now agree that Popoff was correct in his contention, but wrong in his sport's terminology.[14] He simply did not know that Düsselschniffel had invented the *American* football band march, while Olga Pavlov's "football" band march was, in all reality, a *soccer* band march since this is, of course, the Russian word for their own very peculiar type of football.

Now as any competent musical scholar realizes, there is a vast difference between football and soccer—and thus, between the music composed for football and soccer bands. While American football is a dignified pastime, enjoyed mainly by graying businessmen after office hours at the Y.M.C.A., soccer is a vicious, barbaric, and oftentimes cruel display of unabashed professionalism. The latter's players are recruited openly from Soviet high schools and colleges and they are paid exorbitant salaries in proportion to the size of their feet, since soccer is mainly a battle between large feet.

Olga Pavlov was only six months old when her father and mother noticed that nature had endowed the baby with remarkable feet, and her parents assumed quite naturally that she would become a famous organist, acclaimed particularly for her virtuosity on the pedals. Olga was sent to the Kiev Conservatory when she was only six years old to study under the famed organist, Sergius Paginovsky. When she was thirteen, the conservatory expelled her.[15] Olga then enrolled in the soccer program

---

[14] He lived a very sheltered existence as a boy.
[15] For breaking the pedals on their four-manual organ.

at Kiev High School and became noted throughout the Soviet Union for her kicking abilities.

Upon her graduation from high school, Olga was drafted immediately by the Leningrad Tigers of the Soviet League and she was paid a bonus rumored to have been in the neighborhood of 250,000 rubles. She was a sensation the first year (and was named rookie of the year) and led her team to its ultimate victory over the Vladivostok Seals of the Mongolian League.

Unfortunately, Olga got the gout during the summer holidays as Koshoff's famous sketch indicates.

It became obvious that Olga's playing career was over and it was a bitter blow to her, and to Ivan Zubov, owner of the Leningrad Tigers.[16] Ivan, however, accepted it with great equanimity and patting her on the shoulder, he said, "дайте мне водки."[17]

The next day, Olga returned to the conservatory to study composition with Valentine Tolstoy, the famous student of Düsselschniffel's grandson, Hermann, and upon receiving her diploma twelve years later, Olga retired to her estate in the suburbs of Kiev to compose. The first of her 3,407 marches for

---

[16] He wanted his 250,000 rubles back.

[17] This may be translated loosely as, "Good-night, good-night! parting is such sweet sorrow, that I shall say good-night till it be morrow."

soccer bands was finished on April 7 and given its world premiere during the half-time of the game between the Leningrad Tigers and the Moscow Mules.[18]

This great work is too well known for detailed analysis in a scholarly book, but the knowledgeable reader may be reminded that it represents clearly the differentiation between the football band and the soccer band march. The main point of contrast, of course, lies in the overall form of the soccer band march, since it always consists of twenty-two movements and the last movement must be cast as an eight-part fugue with the top line written to be performed by sixty-five muted soprano balalaikas. The rhythmic foundation is, of course, provided by a massed battery of sickle and hammer players. One other distinction should be recalled: the march for soccer bands is always in waltz tempo—somewhat between the English and Viennese varieties.[19]

Nevertheless, the remarkable musical renaissance in the Soviet Union leaves but little hope for the development of this great art in other parts of the world. Myrtle Twichell was *their* hope, but with her passing, America, Canada, England, France, Denmark, Samoa, and other nations have little choice but to translate Russian musical terminology as it becomes available and trust to the profundity inherent in Boris Rasputin's pioneering.

This leads us, of course, to little cheer. There is only one more small bubble of hope waiting for us in the next chapter.

With but one exception, scholars feel that they have been pricked by the fickle bubble of hope and even the exception, Heinrich von Belchergassen, views the future with circumspection: "I cannot sing the old songs I sang long years ago, for heart and voice would fail me, and foolish tears would flow."

[18] The Moscow Mules won 117 to 2 in the overtime period.
[19] According to Popoff, the reason for this is that Soviet soccer players find this tempo easier to dance to.

17

OTHER
DEVELOPMENTS

As there are no other developments in music, the reader is advised to turn back to page one and start all over again with *Pithecanthropus erectus* and his fun-loving prehistoric pets.

But above all, he is advised to remember those famous words written by Dr. Hugo Steinglissinger in the Preface of his collected works:

On with the dance! let joy be unconfin'd;
No sleep till morn, when Youth and Pleasure meet
to chase the glowing Hours with flying feet.

BIBLIOGRAPHY

AARDVARK, OLE, *History of Passion*, Arkansas University Press, 1923.

ABERDEEN, ANGUS, *Phallic Aberrations in Scottish Music*, Glasgow University, Doctoral Dissertation, 1789, Unpublished.

ABDUL-AZIZ, HERMAN, *Geschichte der Turkische Musik*, Cairo, 1901.

BEISSENPFIFFEL, WILHELMINE, *Sexual Aberrations in the Piano Sonatas of Beethoven*, Bonn, 1874.

CAGLIOSTRO, ALESSANDRO, DI, *Storia della Brigette Hissenbaum*, University of Palermo Press, 1791.

CALVERT, HIRAM, *Whiskey and Its Effect on the Minor Triad*, Baltimore, 1629.

CAMBYSES, ABIGAIL, ed., *Encyclopaedia of Sex in Chamber Music*, University of Mississippi Press, 1896–99.

DICKENS, CHUCK, *Poetica Erotica in the Songs of Tiny Tim*, London, 1843.

FESSENSCHMIDT, HEINRICH, *Sexualische Symbolisme in der Pianoische Musik der Franz Liszt*, Berlin, 1879.

GROSSENTEUFEL, KARL, *Sexualische Symbolisme in Wagner's Lohengrin*, Hamburg, 1871.

HERODOTUS, PEDRO, *The Marching Band and Its Effect on the Battle of Marathon*, University of Athens Press, 446 B.C.

HIGGINS, LESLIE, *Sexual Symbolism in Purcell's Ground Bass*, Oxford University Press, 1692.

ITO WATANABE, *Zen and the Working Girl*, Kobe, 1937.

NUSSBAUM, PETER, *Sexual Symbolism in Computer Music*, University of Boston Press, 1960.

O'CASEY, TILFORD, *Immorality in the Violin Sonatas of Haydn*, Privately Printed, Brooklyn, 1926.

SCHOPENHAUER, OLGA, *Phallic Symbolism in Bach's Organ Works*, University of Mannheim Press, 1899.

TROLLOP, BESSIE, *Oedipus Complex and Its Manifestations in Secular Music of Palestrina*, Azuza College Press, 1913.

WHIFFENPOOF, JEB, *Sexual Aberrations in the Organ Music of Handel*, Yale University Press, 1904.

ZWEIFELSMIDT, ADOLF, *Liszt und die arbeitene Mädchen*, Berlin 1901.

ZYGOSIS, FANNY, *Pornography in Electronic Music for Soccer Bands*, Central Kansas College, Doctoral Dissertation, 1959.